"Dear Friend Anna"

Abial Hall Edwards, age 20, in uniform of the Twenty-ninth Maine Regiment, Company K. Taken shortly after his reenlistment in the army and the formation of the Twenty-ninth Maine Regiment. 1863, Casco, Maine. Photographer A. C. Lewis, Portland, Maine.

"*Dear Friend Anna*"

THE CIVIL WAR LETTERS OF A COMMON

SOLDIER FROM MAINE

Edited by

BEVERLY HAYES KALLGREN

and

JAMES L. CROUTHAMEL

The University of Maine Press

Copyright © 1992 by the University of Maine Press

Published by the University of Maine Press
51 Public Affairs Building, Orono, Maine 04469-0150 U.S.A.

First edition 1992
02 01 00 99 98 97 96 95 94 93 92   1 2 3 4 5

The paper used in this publication meets the minimum
requirements of American National Standard for Information
Sciences—Permanence of Paper for Printed Library Materials,
ANSI Z39.48-1984.∞

Library of Congress Cataloging-in-Publication Data
Edwards, Abial Hall, b. 1843.
"Dear Friend Anna" : the Civil War letters of a common soldier
from Maine / edited by Beverly Hayes Kallgren and
James L. Crouthamel.—1st ed.
p.   cm.
Includes bibliographical references and index.
ISBN 0-89101-079-3 (alk. paper).
1. Edwards, Abial Hall, b. 1843—Correspondence.   2. Edwards,
Anna—Correspondence.   3. United States. Army. Maine Infantry
Regiment, 29th (1863–1866)—Biography.   4. United States. Army.
Maine Infantry Regiment, 10th (1861–1863)—Biography.   5. Maine-
-History—Civil War, 1861–1865—Personal narratives.   6. United
States—History—Civil War, 1861–1865—Personal narratives.
7. Soldiers—Maine—Correspondence.   I. Edwards, Anna.
II. Kallgren, Beverly Hayes.   III. Crouthamel, James L.
IV. Title.
E511.5 29th .E39   1992
973.7'092'2—dc20
[B]   92-8232
                                             CIP

Manufactured in the United States of America

BEVERLY HAYES KALLGREN, the great-granddaughter of Abial H. Edwards, received her B.S. degree from Wheelock College in Boston and her M.Ed. degree from the University of Hartford. She is a retired teacher and counselor and lives with her husband in Litchfield, Connecticut. Her strong family ties and interest in things of the past were the impetus to the preparation of this book.

JAMES L. CROUTHAMEL, Professor of History at Hobart and William Smith Colleges in Geneva, New York, is a graduate of Franklin and Marshall College with a Ph.D. from the University of Rochester. A specialist in nineteenth-century America, he has written *James Watson Webb: A Biography, Bennett's* New York Herald *and the Rise of the Popular Press,* and numerous articles and reviews. He is on the editorial board of the New York State Historical Association.

Contents

Preface

There are 113 letters in this collection spanning the years 1861–66, most of them written by Abial H. Edwards to Anna L. Conant, his "friend" and eventual wife. The other letters included are written by Abial to his older sister, Marcia, because in some cases they provide more detailed information than Abial records in his letters to Anna. Documentary information has been derived from the letters, the deposition of Anna Edwards in seeking a pension after Abial's death, the two photograph albums kept by Edwards, and diaries of both parties. Edwards kept two journals, one for 1862 and early 1863, and the other for the 1864 campaigns on the Red River and in the Shenandoah Valley. Each is a terse recording of his location, the weather, significant events, and the receipt of mail from home. (Surprisingly, he notes many letters received from his father but almost none from Anna.) These journals, which have not been included here, are valuable for identifying some of the names mentioned in the correspondence, but they add little to the letters. Anna's diary was for the period after the war had ended. Unfortunately, none of the letters received by Edwards have survived.

The photographs reproduced here, with the exception of the one of General George H. Nye, are all from Edwards's albums. The family papers and albums were in the possession of Abial's son, Philip Waldo Edwards, and on Philip's death in 1909 were saved and stored in a barn by his widow, Chestina Marsh Edwards. The papers were rediscovered by her son Robert Marsh Edwards, Abial's grandson, when he cleaned out the barn following her death.

The letters are in surprisingly good condition. Those written in pencil have faded, but not to the point of being illegible. At some point a philatelist removed stamps from some of the envelopes and took some complete envelopes. Their condition would be perfect had someone not tried to burn them. There was no fire in the barn, so perhaps Anna or one of her children tried to destroy them. It appears as if someone put a pile of them in a fire and at the last minute changed their mind and pulled them out, because it is primarily the borders and folds that are scorched.

The letters are reprinted here as they were originally written. Misspelled words are retained, although they are occasionally corrected in brackets when their meaning may not be clear to the reader. For example, Abial often writes "th" to mean "there"; in the text the word appears as "th[ere]." He rarely used any mark of punctuation except the period, and often his sentences lack terminal punctuation. We have not added punctuation where it was not used; instead, we have separated sentences by the addition of an extra space. Edwards speaks for himself, and there is evidence of growth and improvement in his writing as the correspondence proceeds.

Wherever possible identifying information has been provided in notes for the many friends, neighbors, acquaintances, and relatives Edwards mentions, as well as for historical figures and events. If none appears, the information could not be found.

All of the family papers, albums, and souvenirs sent home by Abial are in the possession of his heirs. These include his autograph album, the McClellan saddle, and a pen used by General Grant.

The editors are deeply indebted to Michael B. Chesson, Marion Remer Crouthamel, Daniel Joseph Singal, and Wendell Tripp for critical readings of the manuscript and helpful criticisms and suggestions. David Ward was helpful in identifying many of the photographs from the albums. Salli Oulette and Dorothy Tibbs assisted in reading and preparing the original typescript. To all of them, thank you.

Beverly Hayes Kallgren
James L. Crouthamel

"Dear Friend Anna"

Introduction

Abial Hall Edwards was born in 1843 in Casco, Maine, the fourth (the second to live past infancy) of nine children born to Samuel Goodale Edwards and Dorcas Caswell Whitney Edwards. During the Civil War, Abial served as an enlisted man first in the Tenth Maine Regiment, and later in the Twenty-ninth Maine Regiment.

Though he was a "common soldier," the diversity of his experiences was remarkably uncommon. After serving in the Shenandoah Valley under the incompetent Major General Nathaniel P. Banks, Abial took part in the bloody Battle of Antietam. He was fortunate in missing the disastrous Battle of Fredericksburg, but he was part of the infamous "mud march" that followed.

Reenlisting in September 1863, after a long home leave in Maine, Abial was shipped to Louisiana as part of the unsuccessful Red River campaign, again serving under the hapless Banks. His luck changed when he joined Major General Philip Sheridan's spectacular campaign to clear the Shenandoah Valley of Confederates in 1864. Abial spent the last months of the war in the valley, and he took no part in Lieutenant General Ulysses S. Grant's final movements that forced the Confederate surrender in Virginia. Until his enlistment expired in 1866 Abial was on garrison duty in occupied South Carolina. For the first time he was able to observe black people closely, and he developed a real sympathy with the former slaves. His letters home contain these and many other observations, including the harsh treatment some soldiers received from civilians when they returned to their homes in the North.

Abial came from a family of enlisted men. His great-grandfather Nathaniel Edwards (1752–1828) served in the Revolutionary War in Colonel Wigglesworth's regiment. His great-grandfather Caswell was also a soldier of the Revolution. A powder horn carried by Caswell in the Battle of Germantown in 1777 has been passed down through generations in the family.

The Edwardses were a closely knit family, devoted to their mother, who must have stressed values of family unity and education. On her deathbed Dorcas extracted a promise from her older children to care for one another and for the older children to help the younger ones complete their education.

When Abial finished his education, grammar school and at least a term of high school, this promise, coupled with patriotism, motivated him to enlist in the Union army. It assured him of an enlistment bounty and an income which he would send to his older sister Marcia, some of which would be used to help his younger siblings. He also worked at the Lincoln Mills, a textile mill of twenty thousand spindles in Lewiston, for a short time before enlisting. It was here that he met Anna L. Conant.

Anna was a direct descendant of Roger Conant of London, England, who arrived in America, probably on the *Ann* in July 1623. He was a planter and governor of the Cape Ann and Salem settlements from 1625 to 1628. He led the first permanent colony of settlers in what was to become Massachusetts Bay.

Anna's grandfather John Conant (1749–1844) also served in the Revolutionary War as part of a 1777 expedition to Rhode Island. Her father Martin (1777–1844) was one of the first settlers of Canton, Maine. He migrated there from Bridgewater, Massachusetts, and worked as a nail maker and blacksmith. Anna's mother, Sarah Knowles Foster, was his second wife. She bore him three daughters, Anna the second. When Martin died Anna was only eleven years old.

After completing school, Anna went to Lewiston to work in the textile mills. It was not uncommon for young women from rural areas to go to the larger towns to board and earn an income. She mentions in the letters being a teacher. It was also common for women who had completed their education to teach the younger children in rural areas. She played the piano, so perhaps she also gave music lessons. During and after the Civil War, until she married Abial in 1869, she apparently alternated between teaching in Canton and working in the mills in Lewiston.

This volume of letters by Abial Hall Edwards joins an increasing number of published collections of Civil War letters and diaries by common soldiers. Until a decade ago, Bell I. Wiley's *The Life of Johnny Reb* and *The Life of Billy Yank* stood alone as studies of ordinary Civil War soldiers based on their own letters and diaries. Now such studies have become more numerous. We have had recent accounts by Gerald F. Linderman, Reid Mitchell, James I. Robertson, Jr., and even one by Michael Barton that purports to be "a quantitative sociolinguistic case study in historical psychological anthropology."

These works, while unable to denominate the elusive "typical" common soldier, have been able to trace common characteristics and themes in the letters home and in the diaries kept by Union and Confederate soldiers.

Abial Edwards exhibits many of these characteristics, and his letters home contain many of the familiar themes. He was young and away from Maine for the first time, witnessing sights and sounds and smells unlike anything that he had experienced before. He expressed concern about the food, the weather, and his physical comfort. He was deathly afraid of military hospitals. He developed strong political views and came to detest the Copperheads, as those northerners who had Confederate sympathies were called. He was anxious about the well-being of his friends from Maine. He was bored and homesick and anxiously awaited the arrival of the mail. It was fitting that late in the war and during occupation duty in South Carolina he became a military postal clerk.

Except for a few written to his sister Marcia, the letters in this collection are all addressed to "Friend Anna" Conant. She became his wife in 1869 following a lengthy courtship (some of which takes place in these letters) that was protracted even after the war because of Abial's family obligations.

In Abial's letters to Anna, the Civil War becomes his personal story. He describes the long marches, the battles, the loss of friends, the plundering, the disease, the cold, the boredom, and the reactions to his regiment's first encounter with black troops. He deplores the incompetency of military surgeons. He evaluates the well-known generals under whom he served, and often his assessments are astute.

He tells of meeting Major General George B. McClellan and other famous generals and of being part of the Grand Review through Washington in May 1865, when President Andrew Johnson and other dignitaries viewed the victorious army, Edwards riding at the head of his regiment with his regimental commander. He mentions seeing Abraham and Mary Lincoln and describes the aura of mourning that pervaded Washington at Lincoln's death. He met Lieutenant General Ulysses S. Grant and got his autograph.

But Edwards's descriptions of the military campaigns in which he participated serve to remind us how narrow was the vision of the common soldier. Edwards knew little of what was going on in other parts of the battlefields, and he often failed to recognize the significance of what he was doing to the broader picture. Rumor passed as fact.

Edwards's education was better than the average education of northern common soldiers. In his letters his spelling and grammar, as bad as they appear to today's readers, are better than in many of the published letters of his contemporaries.

His discharge papers describe him as five feet, eight inches tall with blue eyes, light hair, and a light complexion. His occupation is listed as "weaver," the job he held in the Lincoln Mills at the time of his enlistment.

It is clear that Abial and Anna barely knew each other when they began exchanging letters; Anna was a very casual acquaintance and only one of a number of female correspondents from home. The letters show how the relationship developed through the correspondence into a subtle courtship which ripened into love, although the path was not always smooth. He asked her not to marry anyone until he came home, and she apparently agreed, although at least once she seems to display impatience at the slow pace with which he pursued her. After his discharge, letters not included here show the development of great affection and respect. In one, Abial told Anna that he could have no higher regard for her if she was his sister, the highest compliment. The marriage was one of deepening love.

BIBLIOGRAPHIC NOTE

The classic studies of common soldiers in the Civil War are Bell I. Wiley, *The Life of Johnny Reb* (1943; reissued, Baton Rouge: Louisiana State University Press, 1978) and *The Life of Billy Yank* (1952; reissued, Baton Rouge: Louisiana State University Press, 1978). Recent works are Gerald F. Linderman, *Embattled Courage: The Experience of Combat in the American Civil War* (New York: The Free Press, 1987); Reid Mitchell, *Civil War Soldiers* (New York: Viking Press, 1988); James I. Robertson, Jr., *Soldiers Blue and Gray* (Columbia: University of South Carolina Press, 1988); and Michael Barton, *Goodmen: The Character of Civil War Soldiers* (University Park: Pennsylvania State University Press, 1981). Some examples of published accounts comparable to the Edwards's letters are *Gone for a Soldier: The Civil War Memoirs of Private Alfred Bellard,* ed. David Herbert Donald (Boston: Little, Brown, 1975); Captain Robert Goldthwaite Carter, *Four Brothers in Blue* (1913; reissued, Austin: University of Texas Press, 1978); *A German in The Yankee Fatherland: The Civil War Letters of Henry A. Kircher,* ed. Earl J. Hess (Kent, Ohio: Kent State University Press, 1983); and *Irish Green and Union Blue: The Civil War Letters of Peter Welsh,* eds. Lawrence Frederick Kohl with Margaret Coose Richard (New York: Fordham University Press, 1986). The many viewers of Ken Burns's television series "The Civil War" will be familiar with another New England common soldier, Elisha Hunt Rhodes.

Like Edwards, Rhodes enlisted as a private in his Rhode Island regiment in 1861. Unlike Edwards Rhodes emerged from the war as a colonel in command of his regiment. The difference in the advancement of the two rests in part on Rhodes's education at a commercial high school and his clerical experience and skills, which made him invaluable at regimental headquarters. See *All for the Union: The Civil War Diary and Letters of Elisha Hunt Rhodes,* ed. Robert Hunt Rhodes (New York: Orion Books, 1991). There is information about Lewiston and the Lincoln Mills in George Drew Merrill, ed., *History of Androscoggin County, Maine* (Boston: W. A. Ferguson and Co., 1891).

PART ONE

Maryland and Virginia,

1861–1862

INTRODUCTION

On September 6, 1861, Abial Edwards enlisted for two years in Company K of the Tenth Maine Regiment of Volunteers.[1] The regiment was mustered into service on October 4, 1861. The group left Portland by railroad for Boston on October 6, without arms having been issued, from Boston took a steamer to Amboy, New Jersey, and from there proceeded again by railroad to Philadelphia and Baltimore. Here they were issued muskets on October 21 and began drills. The first assignment was to guard the Baltimore and Ohio Railroad, for which purpose the regiment was broken up into small detachments and scattered. The regiment soon went into winter quarters in Maryland and drilled until spring.

In late March 1862, the regiment was sent to Kearneysville, Virginia (now West Virginia), about twenty miles from Harpers Ferry, again to protect the B. and O. They were there when Confederate General Thomas J. "Stonewall" Jackson launched his successful

---

[1]The company was the basic unit of the Union army, commanded by a captain and containing 100–200 officers and men. (Edwards's Company K, recruited from Lewiston, contained 115 officers and men. His later Company K of the Twenty-ninth Maine contained 125.) A number of companies were joined in a regiment of about 1,000 officers and men, commanded by a colonel. Both the Tenth and Twenty-ninth Maine contained 10 companies. Four or five regiments composed a brigade, led by a brigadier general. Three or four brigades formed a division; two or more divisions formed a corps; and sometimes several corps were combined to form an army. These three larger units were usually commanded by a major general, the highest rank in the Union army except for Ulysses S. Grant, who became a lieutenant general in early 1864.

campaign in the Shenandoah Valley to relieve the pressure on the Confederate armies defending Richmond against Maj. Gen. George B. McClellan's Peninsular Campaign, the attempt to take Richmond from the South, after moving his army to the peninsula between the York and James Rivers.

In the valley the Tenth Maine was part of the command of Maj. Gen. Nathaniel P. Banks, former Speaker of the House, who was consistently out-maneuvered and out-fought by Jackson. Edwards's regiment was always on the periphery of the fighting, doing a great deal of marching and countermarching; after Banks's defeat at Winchester, it was part of the general retreat to the Potomac. Eventually the Mainers went into camp around Front Royal.

Rumors circulated that the Tenth Maine was to be sent to the peninsula as part of McClellan's drive on Richmond. It was not. Instead, it became part of the new Army of Virginia commanded by Maj. Gen. John Pope, a merger of Banks's and two other Union armies in northern Virginia. The War Department had decided that while McClellan's large army was on the peninsula Washington was in danger, and so Pope's army was to provide the necessary protection while McClellan's army was being evacuated and brought back to the Potomac.

This gave the new Confederate commander, Gen. Robert E. Lee, his chance to strike Pope before McClellan could provide enough troops to assist him. Pope tried to unite the three segments of his army, but on August 9, 1862, before Banks joined him, Banks attacked a much larger army, Jackson again, at Cedar Mountain. It is not clear why Banks decided to attack the greatly superior numbers of Jackson. Perhaps it was to try to even the score for his earlier defeats in the Shenandoah Valley. Initially Banks was successful, but then Jackson was able to rally his men, turn back the Union advance, and send it reeling.

The Battle of Cedar Mountain was the first sustained military action involving the Tenth Maine, the time when, in the words of the regimental historian, "the regiment as such fired its first volley." Edwards was in the battle, although he was fortunate that Company K sustained light casualties compared to some of the other units in the regiment.

This was a prelude to the Second Battle of Bull Run on August 29–30, 1862, a disastrous defeat for Pope. "The battle had been fought without us," said the regimental historian. The Tenth Maine had been doing picket and guard duty, but they became part of the general retreat. Still, their baptism under fire had found them resolute, and they gave a good account of themselves. Now they were soldiers.

BIBLIOGRAPHIC NOTE

The regimental history of the Tenth Maine is very detailed and contains a great deal of valuable information: John M. Gould, *History of the First-Tenth-Twenty-ninth Maine Regiment* (Portland: Stephen Berry, 1870). The standard account of the valley campaign is Robert G. Tanner, *Stonewall in the Valley: Thomas J. "Stonewall" Jackson's Shenandoah Valley Campaign Spring 1862* (Garden City, N.Y.: Doubleday, 1976).

Maryland November 16th 1861
Camp Beals

My Dear Sister[1]

I received your letter last night and now hasten to answer it   I thought it very strange you did not write to me but I now see you did not get my last letter from Raymond [Maine]. About our going to Virginia it is a great mistake as we are guarding the Rail Road between Baltimore and Washington. It is a very important point as here is a large stone bridge which all Regiments and army supplies has to pass over in going to W-n   The enemy if they dared to would destroy it as it would help them a great deal. Since I wrote to you I have had a very bad cold and had to go into the Hospital a week   although my cold is better my cough is very bad yet some days I could not speak a loud word   The Docter says my lungs are far from being well and I must be very carefull how I catch cold again. It is a very unhealthy place here. You ask if I am homesick any   No I am not although when I am unwell I think how nice it would be to be at U Southers a day or so   But you tell Jordan[2] if he should come out here he would have many privations to endure that he little thinks of now   He would soon get sick of nothing but cold Bread, Beef, & Coffee. If we want any butter we have to buy it ourselves and cakes ec. but never mind   we shall learn a great deal here that will be use-full in after life   you need not think I am sick of this because I advise Jordan to stay at home but I know he would not like [it]   We all felt much encouraged now as our army seems to <u>just begin to do some thing</u>   The expedition has accomplished a great deal. Our Colonl Beal[3] of Norway [Maine] says he thinks all of us living will be at

home in 6 months But time will show. Ed Shurtleff was in the fleet.[4]
We should have been if we had got our Riffles in season. In about six
weeks I shall have some 20 dollars to send you as I shall have to keep
some to make my self comfortable this winter   Yesterday The[re] was
a Soldier burried near us   It was a solemn sight. first the Drummers
came beating the Dead March (and there is nothing sounds more solemn than that to me) then came the ambulance a two wheeled car-
raige in which the Coffin was placed   then the Soldiers with arms
reversed   after getting to the grave guns were fired over it and the
grave was closed. He was far from home without a Relative near him
to comfort him   he passed away and had to be buried in a land of
Strangers. But our Regiment is not so far from home yet that if any
of us should die our Colonl would send us home. Now about the
affairs in Casco   who keeps the Shadagee School and the Leach H
School[5]   Give my love to Aunt Sarah and tell her to write to me with
you next time   I am pretty well posted on the news in Maine as there
are 3 girls besides you write to me oftener than you do. Tell Mrs.
King I send my love and be a good girl and Ester to Give my best
Respects to Phebe   tell Josie Katie & Philly[6] I shall send some
money soon to get them something to wear. We had a fellow shot in
the hand on guard the other day by a secession Devil   you ought to
hear them talk here   If you ask them how far it is to such a place if
it is a great distance they will say it is "Right Smart Ways" and instead of Yankee I guess so it is "I Reckon so" but enough of this as I
have nothing more to write I will now close Write soon

From yours ec ec
Abial H. Edwards

[*written perpendicular in top left-hand corner*]
Direct you[r] letter to Baltimore the same as ever as we have them
sent to us from there

Abial

Burn this as soon as you read it   I had no good place to write

1. Abial's older sister Marcia, after their mother died in 1855, was responsible
for raising her younger siblings. Abial was three years younger than Marcia.

2. Marcia's husband, Jordan Cook.

3. The regimental commander of the Tenth Maine was Col. George L. Beal.

4. According to Webster's Dictionary, the nautical meaning of the phrase "in the
fleet" may be "on the move."

5. District primary schools in Casco at that time. It is unclear if Abial attended
them.

6. Josie and Katie were younger sisters. Philly was Philip Wadleigh Edwards,
five years younger than Abial. Mrs. King, Ester and Phebe are unknown. No letters
from other young women to Abial have been found.

Relay House[1]
Dec. 23d 1861

Sister Marcia

Having a few leisure moments before the mail closes I thought I would write to you. Saturday night one of our boys died. Greenleaf Herrick of Gray [Maine]. He had a bad cold and the measles   his cold settled on his lungs yesterday. I went and spent the day when he died   It was a sad day I assure you   Last night we got him ready and sent his body home to his friends. Alas what a sad meeting it will be   a few short months ago he left home and friends in the enjoyment of health in the hopes of meeting them again but it was not to be so

It has cast a gloom over our company for he was liked by all   His cousin Nathan Herrick of Poland [Maine] was with him. We got him ready last night about dark to send home and then six of us had to follow him through a dark wood to the depot   It was sad I assure you. After we got him laid out our Lieutenant came to me and said (Abial I want you to take care of yourself   If you dont you will soon lay as he does   I will see you dont do any guard duty nights and commence now and try and cure your cough for I dont want to lose you)   My cough is very bad but I dont feel as afraid as he does about it

I am in hopes next time I write I shall feel better   Write soon as you get this and oblige

Abial

1. Relay House was a guard post on the Baltimore and Ohio Railway.

Relay House Baltimore MD
Head Quarters of 10th Maine Regt
Jan 27th 1862

My Dear Sister Marcia

Having a few leisure moments I thought I would [pass] in writeing to you. I got your letter Saturday and am now looking anxiously for the box[1]

Last week there was one hundred and fifty of our men passed here that had been taken prisoners by the Rebels at the battle of bulls run[2]   most of them were wounded in that battle. The Rebels concluded that it would not pay to feed them any longer and so they released them   They gave us some very interesting information concerning their treatment   They said that the best dinner they got while there was boiled turnips and if you could have seen them you would have beleived their word they gave us a list of their prices in Richmond where they were confined Beef <u>eight</u> dollars a pound common salt twelve dollars a quart Quinine 12 dollars an ounce Tough stories but still we beleive them true

Oh it was sad to look at them one had an arm shot off another a leg another through the eye another shot through his lungs and every breath this poor fellow drew was a short gasp poor fellow his days are numbered and it is a blessing for him that it is so If any one wanted to see the horrers of war all they had to do was to look at these poor fellows. They had rings made of bone that they made of bone to pass away the time one of them sold one of these rings for three dollars as a memento of their sufferings You say you think me extravagant our first Lieut has gone to maine to enlist and I lent him ten dollars for I knew it was in good hands I sent you 8 making eighteen I owed two dollars and bought two shirts as the government shirts were poor for two dollars and it is handy to buy a little butter or milk once in a while

We have got no snow yet to stay and the weather is pretty well mixed up warm and cold a number of our boys are sick with a bad cold They have got the small pox a short distance from here and so our Dr vaccinated us all We have had several spelling schools evenings and it is first rate to help pass away the long evenings I tell you. You ask if Leeroy Tobie[3] is in this Co he is. no more to night. Abial

Jan 6th 1862[4]

My Dear Sister

I now take pen in hand to finish this old letter I have been neglecting it waiting for that box but it has not come yet and I thought I would not wait any longer it must have got delayed as there are two other fellows in this Co that had boxes started the same day so you see am not alone in my disappointment although they are delayed I am in hopes they will be here soon

My health is very good my cough is nearly gone I do not feel it at all unless I walk 2 or 3 miles at a time I thought one spell I never should get rid of it when it got so that I could not speak a loud word even the old Dr when he came to see me used to shake his head but thank fortune it is better Give Miss Ellen Edes my best respects and tell her I thank her kindly for remembering me by her good wishes You said that she had heard letters from me read I hope you do not show my poor letters to any one do you. be sure and not to any more We have been on the road three weeks and in the whole of that time there has not been twenty four hours of fair weather at one time since we have been here   It rains about all of the time occasionally hailing or snowing a little. You can imagine how tough it is to get up in the night to stand guard four hours in the rain better than I can describe. I often think of you as seated in a cosy room before a pleasant fire and think how glad I should be to just make you a call. Ah well no one can tell what it is to be a soldier until they have passed through the mill   But still this is no time to think of personal comforts is it. And if we should live to return we can say that we have done our duty and helped others as well as our selfs. Before I came out here I used to think I was born only to be a burden to others but I have come to the conclusion that I am not quite so bad of for I think I can do something besides being a burden. I had a letter from Phebe last week and have answered it   I was real glad to hear from her. Please to send me ten stamps and I am in hopes that that will last me until pay day as we are to be paid of the 4th of March and I am in hopes to send you more than I ever did before   I had a letter from Alison Shurtleff last week   he said give my love to Cousin Marcia when you write to her   he is teaching their own district school this winter   I have got fifty letters that I have had from Maine since I came out here besides some that I have burned so that you see that I have some letters to answer   I had a letter from Lewiston last night   they said you had plenty of snow and cold weather   Leroy Tobie sends his best respects to you. You may think I am foolish for writeing so much trash but I have plenty of time and I want you to have something to do to read it. I want you to write to me just as soon as you get this and you need not be worried about that box as the express man says that they are often delayed so and I am in hopes to let you know in my next letter that it has come safe and sound.

We have commenced a Lyceum in our Co and it proves very interesting it helps to pass away the time these long evenings   I am in hopes our winter is breaking here as last spring the 14th of Feb they planted their potatoes & Peas here so that you see we shall not have much more cold weather here   It is raining hard now

From your Affec Brother
Abial H Edwards

[written upside down at top of letter]
Do not be at all worried about that box for I shall get it in the course of time   Be sure and write just as soon as you get this and oblige

Abial

1. Evidently Marcia has promised Abial a package from home.

2. The First Battle of Bull Run, or Manassas, July 21, 1861, was the first major battle of the war in Virginia, fought by untried troops on both sides. After initial

Union success, the Confederates counterattacked and drove the confused Union troops into a disorganized flight to the safety of Washington.

3. Leroy Tobie of Lewiston was a private in Company K. Most of the company was raised in Lewiston, where Edwards had worked in the mills.

4. The date of this letter is misleading. The letter is a continuation of the letter begun Jan. 27, 1862.

Kearneysville Jefferson County
V.A. Head Quarters of Co K
Maine 10th Reg⊥
April 16th, 1862

Miss Conant
Dear Madam

I now take the liberty of penning a few lines to you hoping you will not think me to forward in so doing. I have thought of you often since we left the old Lincoln[1] and have often thought I should like to hear from you. I have heard that you were still in Lewiston by the way of our kind friend Laura Powell as I hear from her often by way of letter. It is now over seven months since I enlisted in the army   the most of that time we have spent in the state of Maryland guarding the B & Ohio Rail Road until about 3 weeks ago we came into the state of Virginnia and are now on a Rail Road about 20 miles from Harpers Ferry   the Rebels tore up this Road and the government has just had it relaid and we are put here to protect it from the Rebels and are under the command of. Brigadier General Miles[2] and as he is soon to take a command in the feild we shall be with him   I like a Soldiers life far better than I expected although at first it came hard to be seperated from friends and home and we have to endure many hard ships and privations   yet I believe our cause to be a just and holy one and it is not for us to think of our own personal comfort at this time. Ours will yet be the victory I doubt not. Often since I have been out here I have thought of the old Lincoln and wished I could see you all. and although I did not work there a great while when we seperated there was many friends that I shall not forget   I understand that Charley Additon is in the Maine Cavalry. Is Bill Mace in the Lincoln Mill yet   As I am very buisy to day I will now close hopping to hear from you soon if you think this poor scrawl is worth an answer   please to excuse poor writeing as we have a very poor accommodations to write with.

I remain Very Respectfully
Your Friend
Abial H Edwards

Anna Conant
PS perhaps my name would be more familliar to you as Charley as
you all used to call be by that name

> Please direct to A H Edwards
> Harpers Ferry
> Co K 10th Maine Regt Virginnia

1. The Lincoln textile mill in Lewiston, where Edwards worked until he enlisted, and where he met Anna Conant.
2. Dixon S. Miles, the brigade commander.

> Co K 10th Maine Regt
> Karnysville Virginnia
> May 16th 1862

Friend Anna

I received your kind and interesting letter yesterday and was real
glad to hear from you—and I will now endeavor to answer it

I was glad to hear that the likeness pleased you as you say a Soldiers
life has been very beneficial to my health   for the last four months I
have not seen a sick day. Although I do not know how I shall endure
the hot weather this summer   lately it has been very hot

Doubtless before you get this you will have heard of a
Skirmish that the Maine Cavalry had last Wendsday night at one
Oclock   the[re] was 1500 of our Cavalry surprised by some of
the enemy's Cavalry Infantry and Artillary and they had quite a
fight   two of the Maine boys were killed and some taken prisinors.
One of the Maine Cavalry Companys got entirely surrounded by the
Rebels and had to cut their way through   I got my news last night
from a Maryland boy that was in the fight and was an eye witness
as well as a participater. The[re] was a company of them stationed
here with us   they left here Monday night and was in the fight.
5 Companys of our Regiment is now at Winchester and Banks'[1]
Division has fell back to Strausburg fifteen miles beyond Winchester
and it's the opinion of all that when Bank's advances again that this
Regiment will go with it. Our Captain[2] got here Thursday and he
told of that revival in progress in Lewiston. And I think as you do
Anna about it I think it is everyones duty to lead an honest upright
life and to be a Christian but I think such an excitement lacks the
deep earnest [*remainder missing*]

1. Maj. Gen. Nathaniel P. Banks.
2. George H. Nye of Lewiston.

Martinsburg Virginnia
Head Quarters of Banks Division
Co K 10th Maine
June 4th 1862

My Dear Friend, Anna.

Again I take pen in hand to write a few lines hopping that they may prove acceptable. Since I wrote to you last we have passed through a good deal of trouble but I am still alive and well   But many of our friends are gone. We had orders to leave Kearnysville (where we were when I wrote to you last) the 24th of May. Went to Winchester to reinforce General Banks   we got there in the evening and found that he had only 4,000 men while the Rebels were close [*line burned*] came into town before we left and fired into our Regiment and we were compelled to leave and leave every thing behind even to our Overcoats and Blankets. They drove us 40 miles that day and Oh Anna you can not imagine how much suffering there was   the[y] followed us closely throwing shells into our Regiment   the most of us got to the Potomac that night at 12 Oclock completely tired out having travelled about 40 miles. We crossed the Potomac the next day at noon into Williamsport MD   the next Wendsday our Regiment crossed into Virginia [*burned*] how far of the enemy was after giving four miles we came right onto [*burned*] and we turned to leave and our Co K got seperated from the rest of the Regiment and the Rebels threw a shell and a solid [*burned*] at us and the first thing we knew our own Batteries which went back about a mile commenced fireing at our Company supposing that we were Rebels but luckily they did little damage. But I assure you it did not feel very pleasant to have shells come from each side of us. The Rebels took some of our boys prisinors or killed them   there is only two of our Co missing but there is over 40 from the whole of our Regt   I was completely tired out and if it was not for our Captain I should have been left behind. I can not write you how cruelly they treated our boys they took for doubtless you have seen it in the papers befor this   the Rebels left this place last Saturday and we came here Sunday it is 12 miles from the Potomac   General Banks is here   Our Co is now in a Hall in the 3rd story of the building and General Banks is stopping in a Hotel right accross the street so that I can look out of the window into his room   he is a noble looking man I assure you. We expect to go to Winchester in a day or two and when I get an opportunity I will let you know how we get along   we lost every thing we had that Sunday. Letters, Minatures, ec every thing we had to remind us of home   I am to tired to write much more to day but as soon as I get rested I will write again and endeavor to do better   We have got no letters from home for the last week but we are in hopes to hear from home this week   please write as soon as you get this and direct to

>Harpers Ferry
>Co K 10th Maine Reg
>Banks Division

please excuse this poor apology for a letter and I will do better next time

>From Your
>Affectionate Friend
>Abial H Edwards

>Cedar Creek 4 miles from
>Front Royal
>Quarters of Co K 10th Maine
>June 12th 1862

Friend Anna

Again I take pen in hand to write you a few lines to let you know that I am well and hope this will find you the same. When I wrote to you last I was very tired being the next day after our long march and I doubt much if you can read it. We stoped accross the Potomac at Williamsport one week and one day during the week our Regt was ordered accross the River to do picket duty.[1] We started early in the morning it being the 28th of May (my Birth day) and crossed the River and went to Falling waters a distance of 5 miles   just as we were a going to cross a small Bridge to our surprise the Rebels were a going to cross on the other side of it   our Batteries turned and went back about one mile and all of our Regt with the exception of our Company and we went up on a hill and found ourselves facing quite a body of the Rebels they being but a very short distance from us. We should judge there was over 1,000 of them and there was only 60 of our Company. Their Officer rode up on the hill and waved his sword at us and then they commenced firing shot and shell at us   finding that we could not do any thing there our captain turned us and we were a going to leave the hill when our own Batteries thinking that we were the enimy trying to get around them commenced fireing upon us. and I assure you Anna then we were placed in a trying place   Both Batteries fireing shot and shell at us the shells bursting on every side of us and over our heads but by a great miracle we all escaped the danger   But I must say I never was placed in such a

dangerous place before. We returned to Williamsport that night at
two oclock completely tired out. We have since found out that the
number of men missing and killed in the whole Reg�

 is 15   the[re]
was only one man missing in my Company his name is Leonard
Jepson of Lewiston he is a prisoner. Never shall I forget the day of our
retreat   It was as hot as a July day and the Rebels followed us up very
closely being most of the time within ½ mile of us and never farther
than a mile. We have since found out that they had contrived a plan
to take the whole of our little force prisoners but they took the wrong
road to cut us of and by that means we escaped   They followed us 40
miles that day and I think we were lucky not to loose any more than
we did. The[re] was 4,000 in the whole of Banks force and in killed
and missing there is only 975 the most of them being prisoners   Such a long retreat never was known in this war before and I
hope will not be again on our side during the war   Saturday the 31st
of May we had orders to go to Martinsburg   we got orders to remain
at Falling Waters on picket that night. It rained hard during the
night and our Co had to remain in a clover feild all night   the next
day we heard that the Rebels had left Martinsburg and in the afternoon we started for that place and found that they had left after Rob-
bing the Stores of all the Union men in town. One of the Citizens of
that place that had formerly belonged to the Rebel Jackson Army
took two of our sick Soldiers out in the woods and cut ones of their
throats and hung the other to a tree   Their bodies were found and
buried by the Union Citizens   The man left with Jackson but if he is
ever caught he will fere as he deserves. He took the poor fellows from
the Hospital [*remainder missing*]

   1. Picket duty was the term for guard duty to prevent surprise attacks.

Front Royal Virginnia
First Brigade
First Division
General Banks Army
Company K 10th Maine
June 28th 1862

Friend Anna

   I now take pen in hand to answer your kind letters of May 26th
and June 16th which I did not receive until yesterday. I was much
pleased to get them you may be assured for I had not got a letter from
Maine for Six weeks. As our Mail had been miscarried and we did not

get it until yesterday. I beleive when I wrote to you last we were near Front Royal   we have been in Front Royal doing the advanced Picket Duty for the last ten days. Front Royal is a small town accross the River Shenandoah about 2 miles beyond and as yet our Regiment is the only one that has crossed the River   we have had to go four miles beyond to stay nights so that the Rebels would not surprise us for their Pickets come to within four miles of our own   the[re] is [a] small band of their hated Guerillas is this section of the Country that do considerable mischief   last Monday our Signal Corps was stationed on a hill only ½ mile from the villiage and eight of the Guerrillas came out of the woods right in our sight and fired at the men and then turned and run   luckily they did not hit any one. They tried to catch them but could not. We have indeed been in a hard place this week   our Reg- was liable to be cut of from the river at any moment by the Rebels   at any time they could have done it   they had come with superior numbers. Their Cavalry might have done so as will as not if they only had attempted it. But we were ready to receive them for we sleep with our guns by our side ready at a moments warning. The Rebel force is about 15 miles from here   that is the main body of them   As near as we can find out they have been reinforced and seem to be comeing this way slowly. I think with out doubt that we shall have to meet them before many days and we must leave the issue with God beleiving that he will aid the right and that the Traitors will yet be crushed from the land   It is getting to be very warm, to day especally is almost unberable   already we can see the effects of the warm weather in our diminishing ranks   Our living since our retreat has been very poor indeed (Hard Bread & Coffee) being are principal living but lately our boys has <u>confisicated</u> the secesh's[1] Bee Hives that to such an extent that we have the best of Honey daily and we can get a plenty of the finest of cherries now so that you see we have a few luxuries for all the poor living furnished by government. Charley Additon's company was with us for some time here but now has gone on twords Richmond. I was real sorry that I could not see Charley for I expected that he was here   Our 1st Lieutenant J F Witherell[2] has resigned and started for Lewiston to day   he said he was a going to spend the 4th of July there. I think I should like to be there this 4th. I was in Auburn to a picnic the last 4th but how much differently shall I spend the comeing 4th per chance on the Battle field or in the noisy camp far from home and loved ones   Little shall we have cause for the comeing 4th. My thoughts lately have wandered twords Richmond a good deal   although liable to be called into Battle here at any moment yet I can not help thinking of the many the <u>great</u> <u>many</u> that are now enjoying health that in a few weeks will be lying in a nameless grave   This reminds me of your speaking of your viset to the cemetry and also of your speeking of viseting your Farthers grave   I to have a place made sacred in a country Church yard in old Maine   there is a grave and on the white marble is those words (Our Mother) and it is indeed a melancholy pleasure to viset the graves of our friends. Oh Anna if you could only see this valley   here and there it is dotted with nameless graves some there as that died fighting for their Country lying quietly by the side of those that had raised their hands against it   Even now I can see but a short distance from me. The grave of a Lieut of our army   he was shot by the Rebels the day before our retreat from Winchester   he was shot while standing behind a tree loading and fireing at them and they buried him right where he fell beneath the tree with out a coffin. The tree is pierced with bullet holes where they fired at him   the[re] is over 200 buried here of the Rebel & Union Soldiers that got killed in battle. You spoke of Mr Clarke he is about the same as ever   there is some talk of his getting his discharge and going home soon and shall not <u>miss</u> <u>him</u> much. Thank you Anna for those flowers. Flowers always afforded me great pleasure and comeing so far from friends and home they are doubly dear to me. There is but few flowers here as you can judge by having two great armies in the place   it sweeps every thing away and leaves almost a barren waste. I wrote to Laura shortly after the Battle but as yet received no an-swer   it may be on account of her going to Lewiston. You have in-deed had a great revival in that place and I hope it will do some good if it lasts long. The Adjutent of our Regiment has gone home to get men to fill it up. Those that were captured by the Rebels have been carried to Shailesburg[3] North Carolina   I received that paper that you sent me last night and please accept my sincere thanks   I was glad to get for all it was so long on the way. There [are] many of our boys that even now has not got over our long march from Winchester but as for my self I feel first rate and have got entirely over it   I will now close Anna as I doubt not you will be tired of this. Please write soon for it gives me great pleasure to hear from you. And I will write as often as possible. Give my good wishes to Rhoda & Laura and tell Laura that I shall expect to hear from her soon   Do not fail to write

From your True Friend
Abial H Edwards

PS Please to excuse all mistakes and poor writeing and oblige Charley

1. Secessionists'.

2. John F. Witherell of Monmouth resigned June 26, 1862. Resignations were not uncommon.

3. The Confederate prison at Salisbury, North Carolina, which had the highest mortality rate of any Confederate prison.

Front Royal V-A
Co K 10th Maine
July 4th 1862

My Dear Friend Anna

I now take pen in hand this pleasant morning to answer your kind letter which I received last night. I was so glad to hear from you and to hear that you were enjoying your self so well   Perhaps Anna you would like to know how I was spending the Sunday that you wrote to me. Well I will tell you. Our Regiment for the last 2 weeks has been in the advance of the whole army and has had to do the whole picket duty   our Companys had to go out 5 or six miles every other day and stop all day and night and we found it very tiresome and arderous   Last Sunday we had orders to be ready to march with two day's rations and Sunday morn found our Brigade in line and ready to move. Composed of the 10th Maine 48 New York 5th Connetticut. 28 Penn about 1,000 of Caverly and Battery of four guns we started early in the morning and marched in the direction of Luray Valley   It was very warm indeed in the forenoon and many of our boys were compelled to fall out and about noon it commenced to rain. Then I assure you we had a hard time the soil being so soft the mud was ankle deep in a very short time   It rained constantly until sun down. And we marched to within five miles of Luray Villiage and encamped for the night in the woods   The ground being wet and having nothing but our blankets to cover us we slept very comfortably however within ½ mile of the Rebel pickets. We had orders to form a line of battle the next morning at Six which we did and kept on twards Luray   we marched about two miles and stoped to rest as our Cavarly had drove the Rebel pickets into the villiage and then out of it and they found that the Rebel force had left the place with the exception of a few to check our troops   They drove them from Luray Villiage and our loss was only one Cavalry man killed and two wounded   But Anna I have yet got the saddest part to relate to you   a number of us set down to rest under a tree. Our Orderly Sargaent Frank H. Pratt[1] among the number and one of the boy's gun's accidently went of the ball passing throug Sargaent Pratt's head killing him instantly   It was a sad sad loss indeed to us   he was a noble fellow about 25 years old and he seemed like a brother to us we had orders to return to Front Royal which we did that day (Monday) having marched 22 miles bearing with us the body of our beloved Orderly we buried him July 2nd although we could get nothing but a rough box to place him in and he was buried far from friends at home. Still he had true friends that followed him to his lowly grave A Sermon was preached over his grave by our beloved Chaplain[2] a dirge was played three Volleys was fired over his grave. and there we left as noble a man as ever left home to fight for his Country I received your 2 back letters and paper which you sent me and have answered. the letters directng the letter to Lewiston but I see by your last letter that you have not yet received it I was much pleased to get that paper you sent me and for which please accept my sincere thanks. Last 4th one year ago to day I spent at Auburn [Maine] at a picnic how different this 4th is being spent I did not think this 4th would be spent in the manner it is by me

Abial

1. 1st Sgt. Francis H. Pratt of Lewiston, Maine.
2. Rev. George Knox of Brunswick, Maine.

In the woods Near Front Royal
July 5th[1]

Friend Anna

Again I take pen in hand to finish this. Yesterday while I was writeing to you we had orders to go out and stand picket and so we left camp about four in the afternoon and came out here about 4 miles from Camp and I spent the night of the 4th out in the feild standing picket. I will tell you now Anna this will be a poorly written letter for as I said we are in the woods to day and I have a poor place to write. Last Thursday Company E was on picket where we now are and some Rebel Cavalry came up and they halted them and the Cavalry fired upon them and then turned Co E men returned the fire killing one and wounding two more. and to day our Company stays here until 4 o'clock standing 24 hours. and then we are relieved. We stop in the villiage of Front Royal and the[re] is a rich old farmer living about one mile from camp upon a large hill he has numerous Cherry trees and our boys has made it a practice to go there and pick cherries and yesterday the[re] was eight Rebels went to his house and was a going to shoot us if we went to get Cherries so a negro that belonged to this farmer stole away and came down to camp and told us of it so that Co F went up to lay and Capture them they got most to the house before the Rebels discovered them but they succeeded in taking two of them and bringing them into Camp. One of them we found had been taken before and was let of on Parole of Honor so you can judge how the Traitors keep their word. The Reward for such men is Death and justly to   This place is infested with numerous Guerrillas in small parties that shoot at our pickets and do all the mischief they can. It is said that their is a band of Rebel Cavalry numbering about 700 that is encamped about 8 miles from here. Thank you Anna a thousand times for that Boquet you sent me in your letter. It smelled just as fresh as though it had just been plucket. It caused me to think of times that hase passed and gone in the old "Pine Tree State" whose soil I may never tread again. I had a letter from my Sister and it contained a few verses and I had just read it before Sargaent Pratt got killed to him   two lines I have thought a great deal of since his death it was this. (Do you ever feel as you draw a breath), (That the next may be the gasp of Death")   Never did a few words seem so true to me as that did to see Frank sitting beside us in perfect health and the next second a lifeless corse   not a single breath after the ball struck him passed his lips   Anna I know not where your next letter will find us   A great many thaink that we shall go to Richmond[2] before many weeks   It may be so we can not tell they will keep us where they need us most. It is my opinnion that it will be a hard time for our troops at Richmond. But I can not make it seem that we shall not conquer. how many a home will be made desolate by that terrible battle which in all probabity will be fought before Richmond and already Maine has many a son before that City Ready I doubt not if it need be to offer up their lives for the good of their Country. As you say Anna what a blessing kind and true friends are althoug I think a <u>true Friend</u> is hard to find still when we do find one how we ought to prize them. It is indeed a great blessing to us Soldiers to rec't letters that comes from fiends [*sic*] & home. Many a time have I read & reread your kind letters when I have felt lonely and it always causes me to feel encouraged to read them   you spoke of the loss of your kind Parent   I to have been called upon to loose the kindest of Parents a kind and affectionate Mother and deeply can I sympathize with you in your loss. Anna I will now try and close this letter as I doubt not that you will be tired of so long and poorly written a scrawl. But often when I seat myself to write it seems as though I could write pages such as it is and I hardly know when to stop   please write soon as you receive this for I shall look impatiently for an answer. Please tell me how you passed the 4th. Please give my thanks to your Sister for her many kind wishes and also my deepest Respects. Anna do you remember a year ago this time we were both to work in the same room[3] to gather under the <u>kind</u> <u>instructions</u> of Overseer Treadwell and aid Will Mace   But now how changed many a mile intervenes between us

Please write soon and direct the same as before   I wish I had some flowers to send you but you can judge how few there are when you think of the two great armies that has been in this vally all summer   they have left this place almost a barren waste. Dont get discouraged Anna and think I am never a going to finish this letter for I will now close it as I have got to stand guard soon

From your Affectionate Friend
Abial H. Edwards (alias)
Charly
Co K 10th Maine

Anna Conant

1. Continuation of letter of July 4, 1862
2. Maj. Gen. George B. McClellan's Army of the Potomac on its Peninsular Campaign was close to Richmond.
3. At the Lincoln Mill in Lewiston.

Culpepper Court House
Culpepper County V=a
First Reg First Division
Banks Army
July 25th 186[2]

Friend Anna

I received your letter Monday and was much pleased to hear from you and I should have wrote before but we moved to this place and it took us two days march here and so you see I have had no time to write   we got to this place (Culpepper Court House) yesterday afternoon and found it to be quite a pretty little villiage. Our encampment is on a slight eminence just out of the villiage thus having a fine view of the surrounding country. There is only about 3,000 of our troops here now There has been 7 Regiments of Cavalry here the First Maine amoung the number   They left here two days ago to destroy a bridge over which the Rebels supply passed and they have not got back yet. We are not within [*illegible*] days march of a heavy [*illegible*] of rebels as they hold possession of Gordonsville about 17 miles of this place as their Pickets come to within 9 miles of this place. The rebels have always had possession of this place until two weeks ago. They had cars come to this place for supplies until our Cavalry came here. I think now that we shall remain here until we get force enough here to attack Gordonsville unless the Rebels find out that we have a small force then they might come here to attack us. Anna I almost envy you your enjoyment of home and it's pleasures   now it seems that if I was at home only for a fortnight I should be perfectly happy   I understand that they are enlisting men very fast in Maine. I thought I had no friends to come but I was much surprised to hear that Farther was chosen Captain of a Company and they expects to come in the 18th Regiment. At first I was sorry to hear it but then someone has got to come And it is no use to be selfish in a time like this and if he feels it his duty to come I shall be satisfied. We have been having some very warm weather lately. Anna I want to ask a favor of you   I got my Sisters likeness last week and I would be much pleased to have yours also   Will you send it to me. It would seem like seeing an old Friend to have it. Do as you think best about it Anna and I am in hopes that you will send it. We are now in a place that we can get no news at all and so I suppose you hear the war news long before we do. But as you say it is no use to put any dependance on Newspaper news for they will not tell the truth if they could. For to tell the truth Anna they will cry out a "Great Union Victory" even when we get defeated. I have found it so in several cases. Then in a [*illegible*] to day that 2 or 3 Regiments of us will go on to morrow just to try the force of the Rebels   as yet it is nothing but a rumor. I should not be surprised that we should have a brush with them before I heard from you again   I will now close as I have no more news to write. Please write just as soon as you get this for I shall look anxiously for an answer From Your Friend

Abial H Edward

PS Please direct the same as before and oblige
Charley
[*written on right margin*]
Anna I will endeavor to write a more interesting letter next time

Culpepper Court House
Virginnia
Quarters of 1st Brigade of the
1st Div. Banks Corps
Co K 10th Maine
August 16th 1862

Dear Friend Anna
    It is with the deepest thankfulness to the Giver of all good that I am permitted to write these few lines to you after passing through so

much as we have had to. Dear Friend since I wrote to you last the 1st
Brigade Composed of the 10th Maine 5th Conn—28th N.Y. & 46
Penn—Regts has been in the most bloody Battle of the war.[1] I will
tell you the particulars. Friday the 9th our Reg' had orders to march
in one hour with nothing but gun and equipments. We got ready and
started in that time we marched about 5 miles twards the
Rapidam[2] and stoped for the night as the Rebels had advanced and
their Pickets were close to us we remained in the same position until
noon Saturday having nothing to eat. About noon the Rebel Batteries
commenced fireing which was replied to by our own Batteries they
kept this up until about ½ past four in the afternoon then the
Rebel Infantry came up and our Brigade had orders to advance and
fire at them. This was a solemn time to many Anna for we knew that
some would never leave alive we advanced steadily through the
woods the enimy's bullets flying in all directions until we got into a
feild in sight of them. Then our Reg⊥ advanced with loud cheers the
Old Stars and Stripes flying in our Center. We kept on close to them
their bullitts doing fearful work in our ranks Our Regiment stood
their ground and fought bravely while the enimy sent Regiment after
Reg⊥ and Brigade after Brigade to fight us. When I entered the feild
I never expected to leave it alive but I felt willing and ready if it need
be to offer up my life. Capt. Cloudman[3] Company E stood by my side
and was shot down the first one the fellow that was standing with
me was shot in the face The bullet that wounded him just grazed
my ear causing it to bleed another bullitt passed through the top of
my cap a buck shot through my coat sleeve and still I remained uninjured we were in the engagement just 30 minutes Our Brigade
went into action with just 1,630 men and the[re] was only 811 men
come out uninjured being just ½ lacking four killed and wounded.
The 10th Maine went into action with 480 men and had 176 killed
and wounded. 24 out of the number killed on the feild my company went into the fight with near 20 men out of it th[ere] was 16
wounded 1 killed and 1 missing.[4] General Pope[5] says that it was the
hardest battle of the war The Rebels held possession of the Battle
ground that night and robbed our dead and even robbed the Pockets
of the wounded takeing of the shoes from both our dead and wounded
also stripping our dead Officers of every thing they had on. Oh Anna
the scene is awful beyond description th[e] enimy retreated The
next day leaving the Battle field in our possession They did not even
stop to bury their own dead all of them their loss is far greater than
our's Dr. Garcelon of Lewiston was here and had to work all the
time they are engaged in amputating the legs & arms many a

great many had to loose their legs or arms. Culpepper is one vast hospital [*remainder missing*]

1. The Battle of Cedar Mountain. See the introduction to this section.
2. The Rapidan River.
3. Capt. Andrew C. Cloudman of Portland.
4. According to Gould's regimental history, of 461 in the battle 173 were killed or wounded. In Company K there was 1 killed and 14 wounded.
5. Maj. Gen. John Pope, the commander of the Army of Virginia.

PART TWO

Antietam and After,

1862–1863

INTRODUCTION

General Robert E. Lee, after his defeat of Pope at the Second Battle of Bull Run, decided to carry the war northward from Virginia and crossed the Potomac River into Maryland on September 5 and 6, 1862, concentrating his army at Frederick before dividing it to move against Harpers Ferry and Hagerstown.

Pope's defeated Army of Virginia, or two corps of it including the Twelfth, of which the Tenth Maine became a part, was merged with George B. McClellan's Army of the Potomac, recently returned from the Peninsular Campaign. It too crossed into Maryland, following Lee northward to screen Washington. Lee decided to await McClellan's attack at Sharpsburg, along Antietam Creek, after he learned that Harpers Ferry had fallen to Stonewall Jackson and that Jackson's corps would be able to rejoin him at Sharpsburg.

The Twelfth Corps had just been given a new commander, Maj. Gen. Joseph K. F. Mansfield, a vigorous forty-year army veteran with flowing white hair and beard. Mansfield was an engineer in the old army and this would be his first combat command. He did not arrive from Washington to take charge of his corps from Brig. Gen. Alpheus S. Williams until September 15.

The Tenth Maine, part of the First Division, arrived in Frederick on September 13. They did not participate in the preliminary Battle of South Mountain. The Twelfth and the First Corps, under Maj. Gen. Joseph Hooker, commander of the First Corps, crossed Antietam Creek north of Sharpsburg before midnight on September 16 in a gentle rain, and the Twelfth bivouacked about 2 A.M. on the seventeenth on a freshly manured field about a mile to the left and rear of Hooker's corps.

Hooker decided to attack southward along the axis of the Hagerstown Turnpike toward the Dunker Church. He made no provision for a joint attack with Mansfield, a mile away. Hooker's 8,600 men would attack against an enemy whose strength and position were unknown. Jackson's forces numbered 7,700, as it turned out.

Hooker's attack through a cornfield went well until a counterattack of Confederate Maj. Gen. John B. Hood's division drove back the federals. Hooker finally called for support from Mansfield, and the Twelfth Corps began to move into the cornfield to shore up Hooker's wrecked formations. About one-third of those engaged had become casualties.

The Twelfth Corps consisted of some bloodied regiments like the Tenth Maine and others, about half of the 7,200 who according to Gould, "had never before fired their rifles in anger." They had been roused from their bivouacs as soon as the battle opened, ordered to arms, and had marched toward the sound of the firing, but no one seemed to know what was going on, and there were halts every hundred yards or so.

The troops moved into an open field east of the Miller farm and came under artillery fire, advancing through the debris of battle. They were to form an arc behind Hooker's corps, and Mansfield insisted that they stay in column, to be under better control of their officers, instead of deploying into open battle lines. Mansfield personally led Brig. Gen. S. W. Crawford's brigade, of which the Tenth Maine was a part, to the flank in the East Woods, placing the Tenth Maine where he wanted it. As soon as he was out of sight, however, Colonel Beal deployed his men into the line of battle. The arrival of these massed federals persuaded Hood's men in the east part of the cornfield to pull back.

While Mansfield's men were maneuvering into position, the Confederates were also bringing up fresh troops, positioning them in a woodlot and making them hard to see. As a result, some of the Tenth Maine fired into remnants of Hooker's corps still there.

Then Mansfield was shot squarely in the chest. He was led to the rear and died the next day. Many of his untried men fled from the cornfield and the East Woods. Alpheus Williams, back in command of the corps, conferred with Hooker and plugged the hole Hood's men had punched. They held, and then launched a flank attack. The Confederates fled. The morning battlefield east of the Hagerstown Turnpike was in Union hands.

Over eight thousand had been killed or wounded in three hours. The casualties lay everywhere. About 9 A.M. Hooker was wounded in the foot and had to leave. The Twelfth Corps held their ground await- ing reinforcements, and spread across the field of Joseph Poffenberger's farm, the rebels still hidden in the woods in front of them.

Maj. Gen. Edwin V. Sumner, leading the reinforcements, refused to take the advice of Williams, who was on the scene, feeling that the First and Twelfth Corps were completely used up. Sumner made a disastrous advance based on a misunderstanding of the Confederate positions. The result was a rout, Sumner's retreat finally stopped by a make-shift line in the West Woods, where vicious fighting contin- ued until the Confederates fell back.

Williams and the Twelfth Corps got a call to reinforce Sumner about 9:45 A.M. They suffered heavy losses, but some of Brig. Gen. George S. Greene's two brigades managed to hold a position opposite the Dunker Church. They counterattacked and forced a Confederate flight. McClellan had thrown Sumner's corps into action piecemeal, a tactic he was to follow throughout the day as the battle shifted to the center and the south.

On the northern part of the battlefield both sides had fought them- selves out. At nightfall, the Twelfth Corps remained in the fields in front of the Poffenberger farm.

The battle can be judged a draw. Lee was able to keep his army intact and withdraw across the Potomac to Virginia on September 18 and 19. McClellan did not pursue, feeling that his army had done enough in forcing Lee to abandon Maryland. There had been a great deal of heroism on both sides at Antietam, the bloodiest single day of the war, but the federals were poorly served by McClellan, who was afraid that a total commitment involving all his forces might mean disaster. Not losing was victory enough. Finally, Lee's withdrawal did have an important political result: it enabled Lincoln to announce the preliminary Emancipation Proclamation, to be effective January 1, 1863 (which Edwards does not mention in his letters to Anna). Lincoln had been waiting for a northern victory before announcing the proclamation.

The Antietam campaign was the only time during the war when Abial Edwards fought with the Army of the Potomac. Banks's corps did picket and provost duty around Frederick, Maryland, and later in Fairfax and Stafford, Virginia. They were not involved in any further fighting, including the debacle at Fredericksburg in December, al- though they took part in the infamous "mud march" that followed, and they waited for their enlistments to expire in May.

BIBLIOGRAPHIC NOTE

The definitive account of the Antietam campaign is Stephen W. Sears, *Landscape Turned Red: The Battle of Antietam* (New Haven and New York: Ticknor and Fields, 1983). For an account of the Tenth Maine during the campaign, and until the expiration of their enlistments in May 1863, see Gould's regimental history, pp. 221–337.

Near Rockville M-d.
Co K 10th Maine
Sunday Sept 7th 1862

Dear Friend Anna

I now take pen in hand to try and answer your very welcome letter which I received this week but circustance's have not allowed me to write before. Since I wrote to you before we have passed thrugh a good deal of hard and fatigueing marches. We entered Washington three days ago and came in this direction twords Harpers Ferry   we are about 18 miles from Washington. Drawn up in line of Battle awaiting our foe. It is sad to think that they have entered Maryland but so it is   they have crossed but a few miles above us with a heavy force estimated at 60,000 and are now comeing this way. We have been drawn up in line of Battle ever since yesterday.

In a short time our little Regiment will in all probability be in hard battle but we are ready for them   The boy's are all waiting with a determination to fight and to conquer or die. For a defeat here would be worse than death. We are all pretty well tired out. Our Reg⊥ has been on the march now for 20 day's and in all that time they did not have 3 days Ration's of food and you can judge how they look and feel   twice the enimy had them surrounded but they got away without having to fight but I should judge th[ere] was between 20 or 30 that got tired out and was captured by the Rebels. Many of the troops are almost disheartened by our late disasters   disasters caused by the Traitor McDowell[1] as well as the neglect of other Generals to do their duty   But now the brave McClellan has taken the lead and I hope and think something will be done   as for Pope[2] he has failed to do what he promised us   (Do you wonder that he had lost a good deal of the confidence that the Army did have in him   How matters have changed now our own Capitol is threatened.[)] Last Friday I passed through Washington   I was driving an ambulance in which was two wounded that belonged to our Reg'. I had to stop for over half an hour in the street in front of the White House as th[ere] was a great many teams and ambulances passing as I sat there our President and his Lady rode close by me. I assure you he looks sad and care worn and he looked at the wounded in the ambulances sad enough. He is a very homely looking man but still he looks good his wife is quite good looking I call her. Please excuse poor writeing Anna and a poor letter for you can fancy how I am situated. The teams have all been ordered back out of the way and every thing is ready for the fight which must soon take place here but still I could not help improving the few leisure moments in writeing to you. I doubt not that before you receive this we shall be in another enagement. But I hope we are ready to meet them and if it should be my lot to fall in the defense of my beloved Country I hope to be ready. For it seems as though I never could return home unless we conquer This is the darkest hour of our Country's peril. It is said that it is darkest just before day May this be true for us. I will now close Anna as I shall not have any more time at present Be sure and write soon for your <u>kind</u> <u>letters</u> <u>is</u> <u>so</u> <u>glady</u> <u>received</u>. I will write to you again after the expected Battle is over <u>if</u> <u>nothing</u> <u>hinders</u> Be sure and write soon

Hoping to hear from you soon I remain as ever your ever True Friend

Abial H. Edwards.

Anna Conant.

PS Direct to Washington DC. the same as before and Oblige Charley please excuse writeing materials as it is all I could get.

1. Maj. Gen. Irwin McDowell, who lost the First Battle of Bull Run and was blamed by many for the loss of Second Bull Run, because he commanded the largest corps, which he maneuvered ineptly.

2. Maj. Gen. John Pope, who lost the Second Battle of Bull Run, had bragged about his prowess before the battle.

Maryland Heights MD
Co K 10th Maine
Sept 25th 1862

My Dear Friend Anna

I will write you a few lines while I have an opportunity hopping that they may prove acceptable to you Since I wrote to you last we have been in the severest Battle of the war[1] and thank God I escaped uninjured: we left Rockville and by long and rapid marches got to Frederick the 15th and followed the Rebels up got up with them on the morning of the 16th   the[re] was some fighting the 16th but we did not participate in it   we layed down that night and they got us up about 10 and marched us about three miles and halted us on a ploughed feild close to where our Pickets were fighting all night   we had the privilage of sleeping the remainder of the night on the ploughed ground and got up about 5 in the morning of the 17th   by that time the fighting had become pretty severe   we was marched up a short distance General Mansfield leading our Reg-   we was marched up to a wood the Rebels being in it   then we commenced. It was terrible beyond description   if it had not been for the trees serving as a protection for us our Reg- must have been almost entirely annihilated   as it was we suffered badly. The noble General Mansfield that led us in was mortally wounded and died shortly after. Our Colonel G L Beal was wounded badly also our Lieut Colonel[2] and Major was wounded slightly   out of my Company the[re] was three killed and several wounded. I have not yet found out our loss in killed & wounded but it will be between 30 & 40 killed and many wounded.[3] The Battle raged all day   the bursting of the shells the groans of the wounded & Dying made a scene that was awful beyond description. I hope I never shall see such another   as it is the Rebels are drove from Maryland   we remained on the Battle feild two days after the Battle and had to bury the Rebel dead as the Rebels buried none the them   the sight was awful. I stood on a small knoll and counted 560 dead Rebels on a very small peice of ground. and in another small peice I counted 36 Rebels and 6 of our own men lying to gather. Ah Anna no one can imagine the horrors of a Battle feild until they see it. to see thousands of Dead beings to see Thousands carried of the feild wounded then one can see the horrors of war   the Rebel's loss is estimated at 18 to 20,000 killed & wounded   our loss was not near so heavy.[4] Banks Old Corps was sent here to Maryland Heights and I do not know how long we shall remain here. This place guards Harpers Ferry and I think we shall remain here a number of days. I hope we shall for I am almost sick caused by such long marches and being tired out and such sights as we have had to see is enough to make any one feel unwell. I am in hopes to hear from you soon Anna for I have not heard from you for a long time. Please write soon. I will now close this poor scrawl please excuse all mistakes. When I look and see the many of my friends layed away in their last sleep upon the Battle feild and oh so many suffering in the crowded Hospitals I can but feel thankful that life

and health is still left to me. Have I not reason to be thankful. Anna.
Be sure & write   Direct the same as before.

> This is from your Friend
> Abial H Edwards
> Co K 10th Maine

1. Antietam.
2. Lt. Col. James S. Fillebrown. No major is recorded as wounded.
3. The Tenth Maine had seven killed and sixty-four wounded.
4. The casualties were about equal on both sides, just under twelve thousand,
according to Thomas L. Livermore, *Battles and Losses in the Civil War in America
1862–65* (Boston and New York: Houghton, Mifflin Co., 1901).

> Knoxville, Maryland
> Quarters of Co K 10th Maine
> 1st Brigade 1st Div of Bank's
> Corp's
> Sunday Sept 28th 1862

Dear Friend Anna

I now take pen in hand to answer your kind letter of the 14th
which I have just received. I had began to think you had forgotten
your old friend as I had not heard from you for a long time. As I
wrote to you a day or two since of that horrid battle in which we took
a part on the 17th I will not mention that scene of blood & Carnage
in this. For the last few days I enjoyed a season of rest which a poor
weary soldier only can appreciate. My Co after we got to Maryland
Heights after the Battle was sent to this small town to do Provost
Duty[1]   It is a very small quiet town and <u>so still</u>. I do not know how
long we shall remain here but I suppose that soon we shall have to
follow the Rebels up. I suppose you have read long ere this of the
disgraceful surrender of Harper's Ferry by the Traitor Miles[2] and of
his receiveing as I beleive his just dues his death wound. For I beleive
that the Ferry could have been held against a much larger force than
that that [*burned*] it but we have got it back and I dont think the like
will happen again   Is'nt it discourageing Anna to have to fight the
Rebels and half of our own Generals. There are to many Traitors in
our midst to ever have victory. Often I am almost discouraged. Here
our Army is on the North side of the Potomac with the exception of
those at H Ferry and the Rebel Army is still on the South side of
the Potomac ready to pounce on our army and drive them in to the
Potomac should they attempt to cross and thus the army stands.

Should the army remain so this winter it seems as though the half clothed & half starved Rebels must suffer and leave while our own army is being strengthened. But I do hope that the 1st of January will dawn on a reunited nation but such hopes I think are vain. But is all [*burned*] & the loss of our Friends for nothing I can not bleive it. 3 of my friends fell within ten feet of me in this last dredful Battle while nobly braving the enimy's bullets. Thanks Anna for those autumn flowers for they are dear to me as comeing from a friend in old Maine. You ask if I have heard from Laura lately   I have not heard from her for a long while I do not know what the reason it. You mentioned little Leyman Wright poor fellow he was wounded so bad that he had to be left in Culpepper and was taken prisoner with many other of our boy's   we can but hope he will be exchanged soon. In Co G of our Reg- the[re] was 3 Brothers by the name of Bartlett   one was wounded at Cedar Mountain[3] and had his leg amputeted and died at the Culpepper Hospital. One Brother remained to take care of him was taken prisoner while the last that remained with the Reg- was wounded in the Battle of the 17th and they expect that he will have his leg amputeted.[4] Such war. In such a time as this who can expect to ever see home again. It seemed as though it was a war of extermination more than any thing else. But I will not complain. I will now close my uninteresting letter Anna in the hopes to hear from you soon. For the greatest comfort I have is letters from Friends. If ever I should see old Maine again nothing would afford me more pleasure than to call and see you in your home to which you are so much attached. And no wonder for what spot is dearer than home sweet Home and now Friend Anna Good Night

From your Affectionate Friend
Abial H Edwards

Please write soon Anna
Anna Conant

1. Provost duty involved guarding prisoners of war and deserters.

2. Col. Dixon S. Miles, an alcoholic in command of the federal forces at Harpers Ferry, who was mortally wounded in the Confederate attack. He was posthumously censured by a court of inquiry.

3. Kenneth Bartlett died on August 21 of wounds at Cedar Mountain.

4. Marcus Bartlett died on November 6 of his wounds. Charles Bartlett of Company H was wounded in the leg at Cedar Mountain.

Knoxville M-d
Quarters of CoK 10th Me
Sunday Oct 26th 1862

My Dear Friend Anna

I now take pen in hand to write you a few lines to let you know I am enjoying good health and hope this will find you the same. It has now been a long while since I have heard from you Anna   although I have wrote to you several times since the battle of Antietam I have received no answer from you. But I did not know but what you had wrote to me and like many of our letters been miscarried. We have had no mail for the last week but hope to get our back mail this week   if we do I am in hopes to hear from you. We are still stationed at Knoxville doing Provost Duty while our Regiment is still at Berlin [Maryland]. The army has been lying idle ever since we have been here until within a day or two and by the appearance of things now I should judge that [we] will move this week and I should not be surprised that by the time you get this that we shall be again on the move accross the Potomac. Although I have no earnest wish to cross into Virginnia again if I am called upon I am ready. Oh Anna it is raining hard to day and I assure you it is a lonesome & dreary day in camp life. It causes one to think of the old Pine Tree State and the Friends that are there. Well Anna I hardly know what to write as I have wrote to you all the news in my back letters and I hardly know wether you have got them or not therefore this will be a very uninteresting letter   But if you should get this please write and let me know For I did not know but what you was ill   if so please let me know. I will now close hopping to hear from you soon

I Remain As Ever Your True
Friend
Abial H. Edwards

Anna Conant.

PS direct to
Co K 10th Maine Regt
Washington D.C.
as we hardly know what Brigade we are in now Abial

Point of Rocks, Maryland
Quarters of Co K 10th Maine Regt
Nov 6th 186[2?]

Dear Friend Anna

I now hasten to answer your kind letter that came at hand last night. and be assured Anna It was gladly received for owing to your

long silence I was [in] fear that you was sick but was glad to hear
other wise. As you see since I wrote to you last that we have moved.
we had orders to go to Berlin where our Reg. was stationed last
Friday. As it was there that the most of the Army crossed into
Virginnia on a Pontoon Bridge and the duty was so hard that they
sent for my Co we went to the Regt Friday and remained until
Sunday when my Co was sent to this place (Point of Rocks) to guard
a fort so that spys or any secesh can not cross. But before we came
here we had the privilage of seeing a good part of our large army cross
into Virginnia crossing over the Pontoon Bridge and with loud cheers
they would pass into the woods beyond and here we are far in the Rear
but near enough to hear the cannonadeing daily as our Army
advances I know not how long we shall remain here but I doubt not
ere many weeks we shall be following on through the valley "<u>On to</u>
<u>Richmond</u>" It is very cold to day and it seems much like snow Al-
ready the rain bow colors of Autumn have disappeared in the more
sombre tints of winter Last Monday a week ago as Gen Burnside
Corps crossed into Virginnia he left his sick about 300 of them here
to be sent to Washington and I and 3 others of our company was sent
on the train with them to guard we went to Frederick Monday
night and started for Washington Tuesday morn we got there that
night safe One of the Poor sick fellows died in the cars before we got
there we remained in the City all night and all the next day had a
fine time to visit the Capitol after that I visited the different Hospitals in the City to see many of our Poor fellows that have been lying
there for weeks with severe wounds and some with sickness And
their hearty grasp and glad tones well repaid us for our fatigue Our
Reg has wounded in about every Hospital in Washington we left
Wn that night at dark and got back to our Co the next day much
pleased with our visit to a civalized City The prices you quoted are
indeed monstrous I neve[r] thought that Cotton Cloth would be
that price in Maine. I suppose Mr Treadwell is still hard to work
manufacturing it Did you know that Bill Mace was in the
23rd well he is and now out here some where learning how to soldier. Cant you imagine how he looks cooking his own coffee and what
a face he must wear while eating hard bread <u>Poor</u> <u>Billy</u> How I
should like to call upon you in your cozy home to day But it is no
use to talk of the <u>Cant</u> <u>be</u> so I will now close Please write soon for
your letters are like beams of sun shine comeing as they do in this
drear place

> From you Ever Sincere & True
> Friend Abial H. Edwards
> Co K. 10th Maine

Point of Rocks, Md
Quarters of Co K. 10th Maine Reg⊥
1st Brigade. 1st Division.
Bank's Corps
Nov 9th 1862 Sunday P.M.

Dear Anna

I take this opportunity to write you a few lines hopping they may prove acceptable Tis a cool quiet Sunday Eve. I am sitting in my tent before a <u>small</u> fire in a <u>very</u> <u>small</u> stove. My thoughts as usual are not here but are wandering back to the Pine Tree State. And in the glowing coals I can see the faces of the friends that doubtless now are seated before their own quiet fire sides

(Do they ever think of their soldier friends[)] And to I am thinking of the brave boys that belonged to our Co but the dread bullet has done its cruel work James E[1] was killed at Antietam he was a noble fellow his mother is a widow living in Portland and he was her <u>only</u> son her means being limited he came out in our Co in hopes his pay would help his Mother and now poor woman she is childless God help her and there was Asle R-[2] a hard working fellow of 23 years. He had been to the Acroostook for two years and had got a fine farm from his labors there. And just as our Co was organized he had returned home to Danville to be married to an old school mate and they were to return to Aroostook but times was hard and he got her consent to come out here in hopes to return next spring and with the money he got here to fit up their humble home. But it was not so ordered. He fell on the bloody feild of Antietam close to my side. his blood flying over me in his death struggle. Such Anna is the daily scenes this terrible war presents. If all the agony was confined to the battle field. No there is broken hearts at home. homes made desolate by this cruel war. and who is to answer for this. Echo asks who. There is a very little snow on the ground Friday we had quite a snow storm about two inches fell and it has not yet disappeared. Now Anna who is the smartest in regard to snow we here or you in Maine Anna you said in your last letter that I had great reason to be thankful. Yes Anna I have indeed when I look back and see the great danger I have passed through unscathed I can but say Father I Thank Thee. Lately we have received into our Company 12 recruits from Weld Franklin County. Henry Penny in our Company got a letter from Wm Mace yesterday his Reg⊥ is 15 miles out of Washington doing Picket Duty. As yet he is very well contented Well he might he has not seen the hardships of a soldiers life yet We have heard that the 7th Maine is to be filled up and is to return soon is it so The most of

the Army is on the move   Th[ey] must have suffered much during
this late snow storm. Especially the bare footed Rebels. There is every
prospect of another great battle being fought soon   if it was not
americens in both sides we might hope it would be the last but as it
is neither side will acknowledge them selves beat and I for one never
want to see the Federal Army acknowledge it   And I think they
never will have to   Well Anna I will not write any more to night as
doubtless you will be tired of this so I will now close by wishing you
Good Night

Affectionately Your Friend
Abial H. Edwards

1. James Eaton of Company K.
2. Asa Reed of Company K.

Point of Rocks Frederick Co. M-d
Quarters of K Co.
10th Maine Regiment
Nov 12th 1862

Dear Friend Anna
    We have just received our mail to night and I was much pleased to
receive your kind letter of the 6th. For this is just such an eve that one
would like to hear from friends   It commenced raining this afternoon and it now has the appearances of being a long storm. if there
is any thing that makes me feel lonely it is a long rainy evening and
it is now just the season that we must expect many such. To day has
witnessed the burial of another one of our Reg⊥ he died of fever his
name was Mathews.[1] Last week th[ere] was two died also   There is
now quite a number of cases of Typhoid Fever in our Reg⊥ there being
three in my Company   Colonel Beal is here with us   his wound is
now entirely healed. I suppose e're you receive this that you have
heard of the removal of Gen McClellan and of Burnsides[2] taking his
place. how do the people in Maine like that. For my part I am much
pleased with it. While my Co was stationed at Knoxville it was my
lot to see both Generals often as I have wrote to you before and often
with their wifes   As for McClennan he always looked pleasant but
still he lacked a certain way which Burnside had of commanding
respect. And the reason he was liked so well by his army is because
he was so kind to them not because he was a great General. As for
General Burnside I always liked his appearance much   he looks as
though he is a man that would fight. (And the past has proved it)

always looking out for his men—and the Corps that he has always commanded thinks as much of him as McClellan troops thought of him and besides McC- is to slow and it is the belief of all that Gen Burnsides will still push on and that again the cry will be "Onward to Richmond" I have only spoke of my own opinnion of the removal. Gen McC- has been a good Gen to th[e] Army but we need something—more. And I think for one that it is for the best, time will show. You say you are enjoying good health with the exception of a severe cold. That is just like me for I have a bad cold indeed Only think Anna you weigh almost as much as I do I weigh 154 but never mind when I get to Maine I shall soon tip the scales to 170 per-haps. I can but echo your wish that the 1st of Jan next will dawn on a reunited people. But I fear it is useless to wish so for this bloody war will yet have to see some of its hardest fought Battles in the year to come I fear for our Army still moving on twards Gordonsville. As yet none of our Army has gone from Harpers Ferry twords Charlestown & Martinsburg As they all went by the way of Berlin so that the Rebel Pickets come to within a short distance of the Ferry. And as our main Army is now in the rear of them I suppose that our folks are waiting for the Potomac to rise so that they cannot cross and then for us to drive them twords Winchester and our main army come up in their rear. That is all the reason I can think of for leaving them quiet so long. You ask if I ever heard from or seen my Farther since he joined the Army. Fortunately (I think) he was taken sick in Portland and resigned not being in service but about two weeks he is now quite well. You asked about E. D. Clarke he was detached from the Regt last spring to work in the Government Rooms in Baltimore [*remainder missing*]

1. Charles Matthews of Company G, who died of consumption on November 12.

2. Maj. Gen. Ambrose E. Burnside, who replaced McClellan as commander of the Army of the Potomac on November 7.

Point of Rocks
Frederick County Maryland
Quarters of Company K
10th Maine Regiment
Thanksgiving Day Nov 27th 1862

Far distant yet Ever Remembered Friend Anna

Your thrice welcome epistle of the 16th is before me and be assured I was right glad to hear from you. I got your letter last night and though it came the day before Thanksgiving. Yet it was as acceptable as a good Thanksgiving dinner

[*burned*]

great blessing to commune with Friends Through the silent language of the pen. The letters I have received from friends have in a great measure help me pass through the toils & Dangers of a Soldiers life with far more fortitude then though I did not receive those <u>precious</u> Epistles. One year ago to day we had a splendid dinner sent us from Lewiston and we enjoyed ourselves much. But circumstances are such now that they cannot do so this year   But I doubt not they think of us often during this day. May you all have a pleasant day. I feel indeed thankful that life, and in a great measure health has been mine during the past year. While <u>so</u> <u>many</u> of our brave boys that were with us one year ago to day are now at rest. I trust the crown of glory is theirs and we should not mourn for them. It is very pleasant to day a warm sun it is indeed a pleasant day may you have such in Maine. We have had some Rebel Cavalry as near neighbors lately but they have not troubled us and if they do I think they will find K ready to meet them. I received a letter from Farther yesterday   I was surprised & pained to hear that he was married. My own Mother has been dead now six years but it has always been my wish that her place might never be occupied by another, a stranger [*burned*] so far forgotten [*burned*] prejudice as to write and wish Farther happiness. but still it seems hard. It is very sickly in our Regt another member was buried yesterday I was very unwell last week and the Doctor thought I was threatened with a fever but Thanks I am almost well. I have not much news to write to day Anna and so I will now close   Please write as soon as you get this for you know [*burned*] the pleasure it gives me to receive your nice long letters. When I feel rather <u>blue</u> as the boys call it your letters always dispel all gloomy thoughts.

I remain as ever your Friend
Anna Conant x Abial H Edwards
Co K 10th Maine
Point of Rocks Maryland
Please direct so

Near Fairfax Station Va
Quarters of 10th Maine 1st Brigade
1st Division 12th Army Corps
January 5th 1863

Dear Friend Anna

I take this opportunity to write you a few lines hopping that they may prove acceptable

I received your kind missial of the 7th ult <u>last</u> <u>week</u> but not until I had sent a letter to you directed to Canton as usual. We still remain where we have been for the last few weeks and had got [*burned*] When on the night of the 27th our Reg⊥ had marching orders and our whole Division started twords Dunifries' early on the 28th I did not go however as I was acting Clerk in the Reg⊥ Post Office and we some expected a mail in that afternoon and I was left to take care of it The Reg⊥ took nothing with them leaving the sick and tents here after our troops had got out about 5 miles th[ere] was a squad of Rebel Cavalry about 1,200 came in between our men and the camp and they destroyed one Regts camp a short distance from here and we expected them here in camp so much as could be. Capt. Emmerson[2] remained here with us and we all got our muskets ready to give them a slight welcome but by some means they got frightened out of paying us a visit and instead [*burned*] around us [*burned*] some of the time they was within a mile of our camp. Gen Geary[3] Division had a small fight at Dunifries but our Division did not get there to help him our boys heard that th[ey] had come and destroyed our camp and taken us prisoners and when they was ordered back to camp in the afternoon the[y] expected to find nothing but ruins. But thy [*sic*] was much pleased to find all "Quiet in Camp" On the next morning they was again routed up at 2 A.M. and was marched out to some Rifle Pits and remained there until 10 A.M. but as no Rebs showed themselves they came into camp since then all has been quiet we are now having some delightful weather the almost too good to last long we have no snow. We have all of our tents loged [logged] up from three to four feet and in many of them fire places thus making them far more comfortable. But it is uncertain how long we shall remain here we may leave any day and may not for weeks I have now been Clerk in our Regimental Post Office for two weeks but I donnot think I shall be so long for I had much rather be with the company even if the duty is harder Well Anna I suppose that by this time you are <u>comfortably</u> settled in a boarding House Please let me know how you enjoy yourself. By the way I saw Cloe Buck's[4] marriage in a news paper   is she really married

Please write to me soon and write me all the news and how Old Lewiston looks now if the same as ever   He. He. Please excuse Poor writeing

> I Remain as Ever Your True Friend
> Abial H. Edwards
> Co K 10th Maine Reg⊥

Anna Conant.

1. Dumfries, Virginia.
2. Charles S. Emerson.
3. Maj. Gen. John W. Geary.
4. Clorinda Buck.

> Near Fairfax Station,
> Fairfax County Va
> Quarters of 10 Maine Reg-
> 1st Brigade 1st Division
> Slocums 12th Army Corps
> Jan 10th 1863

Ever Rembered Friend Anna

With pleasure I take pen in hand to answer your kind and eagerly watched for missive which I received by to nights mail. It has been raining all day and it is just such a day as that soldier ought to receive letters from friends for to me a letter from a friend pays for the disaggreeable day. Anna I was much pleased to receive your nice long letter. I have been anxious to hear from you for a long while and had almost come to the conclusion that you had forgotten me   The last week has been very uninteresting here   nothing of interest occured with the exception of good news from the west[1]   It is indeed encourageing to hear such glorious news from there even if we cant see any thing done here   Still Bitter must always be mingled with the sweet   It is sad to read the account of our defeet at Vicksburg[2] to read the account of 6000 more of our poor fellows being killed and wounded and all for nothing. But Oh may the time soon come when such defeats will be of the past not the present   Yes Anna our term of service expires the 3rd day of next May   we have now only about 3 and a half more months to serve before we can again see Home and Friends once more. It has been a <u>long</u> <u>long</u> while since we have had that pleasure. Even now one can hear the principal topic of conversation in the Reg- about the time that we are to go home   This Mr

Wright[3] you spoke of is 2nd Lieutenant in Company H of this Reg-
Company H is the Auburn Co   Our Regiment is the only 2 years
Reg- from Maine. You spoke of E D Clarke being at Home. He belonged to my Co but has not been with us during the past summer.
I beleive he was to work in a Hospital in Baltimore and he got his
discharge from there. You spoke of Clorinda Buck   I saw her marriage in a newspaper   she was indeed a nice girl. I should think as
you say that all the girls in Maine are makeing the most of the
time while we are away   I think that when we get back we shall
stand a <u>small</u> <u>chance</u> Dont you

I expect Anna that when we do return that we shall be a lot
of uncouth fellows that have forgot all that we ever did know of
civilized life for I think that we have lived during the past 2 years
in a land of Barbarians and you must not be surprised at the
change it has made in us   I often think if our friends at Home
have changed as we have. But never mind Anna if we have grown
rough and weather beaten   we shall have the same warm hearts
to greet our friends and the past seperation will only teach us the
value of Friends

I should like to be in Lewiston some of these fine evenings and see
you all enjoying your self in skateing. I should think that the young
people of Maine were enjoying them selves finely this winter. I am
glad that they do certainly. But never mind I shall be at home in
season to help gather the berries. Shant I   To remain a few weeks
with the loved ones and then if need to try the fortunes of war once
more for I think it is the duty of one and all to spend their lives if it
need be in crushing out the foul nest of traitors that have been such
a curse to our land. No more to night

Abial

Sunday Jan 11th 1863

Dear Friend

I will now take pen to finish this poor letter[4]   It has cleared of fine
and still rather cold. I have just been out and by the way I heard a
little Robin singing his pretty tune. It sounded sweet to hear the little fellow in mid winter   Please give my sincere Respects and Esteem
to Laura Powell

Our Adutant 'Shaw'[5] of Lewiston arrived here to day   he has not
been with us for many months has [*sic*] he has been at home Recruit-
ing for this Regiment. By the way Anna I dont want to hear of your
being married until we get back for I shall want a Sister[6] to go and
see in Lewiston and if you was married your Husband might object to

it   So I shall want your promise to remain <u>free</u> until then. That is if you can give it willingly

Well Anna I will now close my poorly written letter and I will try and do better next time   And I also wish to put this in the next mail

Please write soon for I am always anxious to hear from you

Yours with Friendship Ever
Abial H Edwards

Anna Conant

1. The Union victory at Stones River (Murfreesboro), Tennessee, on December 31, 1862–January 2, 1863.
2. Maj. Gen. William T. Sherman's unsuccessful attempt to take Vicksburg, Mississippi, from the north in December 1862.
3. 2d Lt. Horace Wright.
4. Completion of letter begun on Jan 10, 1863.
5. Elijah M. Shaw.
6. Sister is used here in a common usage of the time, "Sister" (or Brother) in Christ.

Near Fairfax Station,
Fairfax County, Va.
Quarters of 10th Maine Reg⊥
1st Brigade
Jan 14th 1863

Dear Sister Marcia

I will take a few minutes now to drop you a few lines   We are now under marching orders with the prospect of leaving here in a very short time. They have been very buisy drawing Rations etc. showing that we shall leave soon. Where our destination is we do not know probably to Reinforce Burnsides   We can but look forward to this march with feelings of regret. It is cloudy with every appearance of rain and to march through the mud, to sleep on the cold damp ground with out tents (For we havent teams to carry our tents) is not very encouraging to us. We have now been working for months for government endured every thing with out the pay that was due us and a great many have families at home that need their pay. Do you wonder that they are dissatisfied that the Soldier is disheartened, discouraged. If the government wants Soldiers that is ready to do Let them treat them as men not as Brutes. I do not feel as dissatisfied as some do and I dont feel as though I had reason to be   But still it is grinding to me as well as the rest

Well Marcia in all probability we shall leave here certainly by to Morrow. I will write to you often and let you know where we are etc.

45

etc. And don't you stop writing for we shall get our Mail just the same. Our Chaplain is gone and I have had the whole charge of the mail is on me   I dont like it very well but have to take care of the Post Office until he Returns   Well Marcia I will now close   Be sure and write often   From Brother Abial   Direct the same as before   And now may the Great Spirit Watch over us all and be with us in all the trials that we shall have to undergo

Abial H. Edwards

Co K 10th Maine

Marcia you recollect that cap that had a bullet put through it   as I can't sent the whole of it I will send you the piece the ball passed through   it was the top of the cap   It hit the peice hevy and I tore it out. Nate Herrick[1] had a ball put through his cap at the same time   I never looked at it without a shudder to think how near death came.

A H E

1. Pvt. Nathan Herrick of Company K.

Near Fairfax Station, Va

Quarters of the 10th Maine Reg⊥

Sunday P.M. Jan 18 1863

My Dear Friend Anna

With pleasure I devote a few spare moments from the bustle and noise of preparations to move to write you a few lines hopping they may prove acceptable. It has been very buisy with us for the last week in prepareing to move and we have had several orders to move which has been countermanded but with out doubt we leave here to morrow   Where our destination is we know not   all is we can but hope that it will not be much worse than it is here. We are having some fine weather now but still very cool nights which will be very sever on us to be compelled to sleep in the open air   But what we have endured once we can again be it ever so hard   I think it fortunate for us that we have no snow.

Our Reg⊥ was paid 4 months pay yesterday and our Chaplain Mr. Knox leaves here for Maine to morrow to carry the money home for the Regiment. I doubt not his comeing will make many a glad heart in the Old Pine Tree State. For many have families that in a great measure depends upon the monthly pay of Husband and Farther for a living and it has now been nearly 7 months since the next to the last

payment   Mr. Knox will be likely to spend a few days in Old
Lewiston. I have charge of the Regimental Mail while he is
gone   not a light duty but still very easy on a march   Anna I will
write to you again as soon as we reach our destination   I think that
we shall not have many days marching to do

I dont know Anna but what I tire you with so many letters but I
could not resist the temptation too write   Hopping to hear from you
soon I Remain As Ever

Your True Friend
Abial H. Edwards
Co K 10th Maine
Washington D C

Anna L. Conant

Stafford Court House. Va
Quarters of 10th Maine Regt.
1st Brigade. 1st Division,
Slocums, 12th Army Corps
Jan 26th 1863

My Dear Friend Anna
I will now take pen in hand to write you a few lines hopping they
may prove acceptable   As you see by this we have moved again. We
left Fairfax Station on the morning of the 19th the same day that our
Chaplain left for Maine. The day that we commenced our march was
fine and cool and we expected some fine weather   we marched about
8 miles the first day and then encamped on the Dumfries Road. The
night was very cool and the ground damp and as you may suppose we
did not pass the night very pleasantly

The Country through which we passed is the most desolate
gloomy looking that I have yet seen. On the 20th we marched about
10 miles and camped at Dumfries for the night. It commenced
raining during the evening and rained steady all the night and
as we could do no better we had to sleep on the wet ground. On the
21st our Reg- was acting as Rear Guard on the ammunition train   it
rained hard all day and the mud was so deep that the horses could
not haul the ammunition up the hill and so we had to carry it up on
our own shoulders   We worked hard all day in the rain with out any
thing to eat and at night we had got just one half a mile. And another
rainy night we had to endure on the cold wet ground with nothing
but our thin shelter tents and the boys had to go supperless to

bed On the 22nd we marched about 8 miles and at night my
company was on Picket during the night on the 23rd we marched
about 5 miles and got to this place pretty well tired out I assure you.
The storm did not clear of until the 24th. And now it has cleared
of warm and fine. I often thought during the long tedious march
that if those at home that was a scolding about the slow movements
of the army could have been with us during that march and have
seen the roads and seen the dead mules and horses I think they
would have favored winter quarters and let the poor soldiers
alone. God knows I wish this cruel war was ended but Anna one
thing is sure nothing can be done durng the winter months. More
will be killed by exposure and such marches as this than will be
killed by the Rebels bullets. General Sigels' Head Quarters is at
this place but the most of his troops has gone on. It is now warm and
fine but it will be a long while before the mud dries up. Yesterday
and to day the Robins sing right merrily and I assure you it sounds
pleasant. I think now that we shall remain here for some days perhaps
weeks We are now fifteen miles from Fredericksburg and about
eight miles from Falmouth which place is Gen Burnsides Head
Quarters. I now think that the next time the army moves that we
shall be with them but I think it will be impossible to move for a
number of weeks yet

Havent we been fortunate Anna in not having any snow this
winter for we should have suffered far more than we have yet. But
still there is some chance to have a little snow yet. We have now
been here 2 days and already we have got some log huts built up
with fire places in them. We find them far more comfortable than
the small tents and we find that they pay for them selves even
if we dont remain here but a week. If you see Laura Powell Please
tell her I got a letter from Charley Huston in the 23rd Maine
yesterday he was well and he spoke of Bill Mace. I should judge
by the letters that Bill sends to Henry Penny of that company
that he is home sick enough but one thing is sure the 23rd has
always had a very lazy time and doubtless will have as long as they
are in the service. Our Regiments time expires as you know on the
3rd of next May

We have had a great many recruite that enlisted for 3 years and
now in the Reg- th[ere] is about 375 men for duty and out of that
number the[re] is 252 recruits or 3 year men. And now they say that
there is a prospects of discharging the old members and filling up the
Reg- with 3 years men but one thing is sure I think I shall go home

and have a short rest. But now I will close Anna for fear that I shall tire your patience.

Please Write just as soon as you get this and oblige Your
Ever True Friend
Abial H Edwards

1. Maj. Gen. Franz Sigel.

Stafford Court House V-a
Quarters of 10th Maine Reg⊥
Febuary 6th 1863

My Dear Sister Anna.

i now take pen in hand this quiet evening to answer your very acceptable letter of the 1st which arrived safely to day. You know not with what pleasure your letters are read and how eagerly they are watched for. Would that I could receive them oftner. The most of this week has been very lonely indeed as it has stormed the most of the time but it has cleared of cool and pleasant. But such travelling you never saw   It commenced to snow and about six inches fell when it turned into rain and rained two days leaving us truely speaking stuck in the mud.

But still we must be contented   the time is passing away fast within three months we shall have the pleasure (God permitting) of once more seeing the shores of the sunrise state and of clasping the hands of the friends from whom we have been so long seperated and I hope to see Sister Anna among the first to meet me. Lewiston will be my first stopping place and perchance a permanent one. but still I can not decide yet. I often think of home and and never without thinking of you. It gives me great pleasure to hear of your enjoying yourself so well this winter. I neve[r] enjoyed my self so well from home as I did in Lewiston but I expect that the place has changed much as well as the people for 2 years will change the people as well as the place. You spoke of our Chaplain being in Lewiston and of preaching there   he is a <u>noble</u> <u>man</u> and I think a <u>true</u> <u>Christan</u>. Never did I get acquainted with a Minister that I think more of than I do him   If you went to hear him preach I doubt not you liked him. He was as cool on the battle field as he is in the pulpit   when shells was bursting around his head at Cedar Mountain he was with us speaking a kind and encourageing word to all. He has the love and respect of all the Reg⊥. Our Regiment has considerable Picket duty to do at this place   My company goes on Picket about once in three days and remains 24 hours   it is rather rough during these snow and rain storms where in many places they do not allow fires   The[re] was quite an accident happened to our Cavalry Pickets last night   the 14th Penna- Cavalry was on Picket about three miles from here and last night at dark the[re] was a lot of Rebel Cavalry surprised them captureing 17 of our men with their equipments. and horses and killing two of our.   none of the Rebels was hurt   So you see that even if it is so muddy we have occasionally a visit from the grey backs. We have now a prospect of fine weather and I hope it will continue so. I will now close this <u>very</u> uninteresting letter Anna for I am almost ashamed of it. Please write soon Anna and oblige Brother Abial.

Hopping to hear from you soon I will now close by wishing you lots of pleasant times this winter

As ever your True Friend & Brother.
Abial. H. Edwards.

Anna L. Conant.

Stafford Court House.
Stafford County. Virginnia
Febuary 8th/1863

My Dear Friend Anna

With pleasure I seat my self to answer your kind letter of the 8th which came to hand last night. I was real glad to hear from you as I always am. Anna we are now having some lovely weather just cool enough to be pleasant for exercise

They tell us Anna that there is now a prospect of our being sent to the rear. to Baltimore or the Relay House to serve out the remainder of our time. Our Colonel[1] as you know was badly wounded at Antietam so that it has unfit him for active service hereafter. And he told the General that if they wished him to remain with his Regiment they must place us some where where we would not have to march. And he got the consent of Colonel Knipe[2] who commands our Brigade also the name of General Williams[3] who commands our Division and the consent of Major General Slocum[4] our Corps Comander and also the name of General Hooker.[5] and now all he wants is the consent of General Hallock[6] before he could get that he was taken worse and had to go home. and now Our Lieut Colonel J S Fillebrown has gone to work. General Slocum gave him leaf of Absence for ten days and he has gone to Washington to see Gen Halleck and now we are waiting anxiously for his return. We hear that General Scheneck[7] who commands at Baltimore that he has offord a full Regiment of 1200 men to Slocum for us and we are in hopes it is so   if so we shall either go to the Relay House or Baltimore. But we have got to wait and hope for the best. Oh Anna Our Chaplain has got back he came to night you may be assured that we was glad to see him. He says that he has enjoyed himself finely in Maine.

Anna you have given me quite a compliment by asking me to write for your paper. Willingly would I do so Anna if I could. I will now give you my reasons and hope they will excuse me as I think they will. It has now been two years as I might say since I have mingled with civilized people (I dont mean my Reg- but the people of Vir) and I must plead ignorent of the principal topic of the day. and it has been so long since I have looked inside of a grammer that my composition would be worthless therefore Anna I think you ought to excuse me (Wont you please.) Tis a splendid evening quite warm and as I sit here writeing the music of splendid band comes to me borne upon the still night air. They are seranading General Hooker who stops to night with General Sigel about one half a mile from here   What sounds more noble then to listen to a splendid band on a quiet still evening

I now expect that the Captain of my Company (Capt Nye)[8] will be appointed Major of the Reg- as he has been elected by the Officers. This fine weather is fast drying up the mud and if it should continue fair for two weeks longer we shall probably have dry roads and perchance a <u>grand</u> <u>move</u>   we may be in it and then again may not   now it seems very uncertain. General Burnsides Old Corps has taken transports here at Aguia Creek and gone to Fortress Monroe. The 2nd Division of our Corps (12th) has also gone to Aguia Creek it is thought to take transports. If they do I think that our Division (General William's) will also go on some expedition but a few days will decide wether we shall go to or be send to the rear and another Reg- take our place. As it is getting late I will now close. Please write soon and write often

> From Your True Friend & Brother
> Abial H Edwards
> Co K 10th Maine

1. Col. George L. Beal was wounded in both legs at Antietam.

2. Col. Joseph F. Knipe was, at the time of this letter, a brigadier general in the Army of the Potomac.

3. Brig. Gen. Alpheus S. Williams.
4. Maj. Gen. Henry W. Slocum.
5. Maj. Gen. Joseph E. Hooker, who had replaced Ambrose Burnside as the commander of the Army of the Potomac.
6. Maj. Gen. Henry W. Halleck, general in chief of the Union armies.
7. Brig. Gen. Robert Schenck.
8. Col. George H. Nye.

> Stafford Court House.
> Stafford Co., Va
> Quarters of 10th Maine Regiment
> Febuary 22nd 1863

Dear Friend Anna

Your kind and thrice welcome letter of the 15th is before me and right glad was I to get it. Tis a wild stormy day a real old Maine snow storm is covering us and promises well to fairly bury us in snow. Yesterday was a lovely day warm and pleasant. But last night it commenced snowing and has continued since then   already two feet of snow has fallen with fair prospect of much more. Tis a rough looking camp scene this the little huts almost buried in snow and every crevice the snow comes blowing in soon giving us a pretty good supply of snow outside and in. But in all of this tempest some one is to work as we can tell by the boom of the cannon. As yet we can not find out the cause of it wether it is a Salute in honor of Washington's Birth day or wether it is to shell out the Rebel pickets probably the first however. Oh Anna that most dreaded of all diseases the small pox has broke out in our Regiment   a young fellow belonging to Company G lately returned here from a Hospital in Alexandria and after reaching here was taken sick with the small pox   But every thing has been done to prevent the disease to spread far in the Reg⊥   They have built a Hospital some distence from the Reg⊥ and they put those sick into it   But for all that it will spread throughout the Reg⊥ it is a fatal disease and I have always dreaded but it is no use to be discouraged about it for it will be no worse for me than for the others

Tis evening the "tatoo"[1] has been beat throughout the different camps and nearly all have retired. No not all for there are many on guard and out on Picket to night with nothing to prevent the cold wind and snow from blowing about them. Little do our friends at home realize the hard ships of camp life   But like all of our past troubles it will soon pass away and we can look back upon

our sufferings with a smile. My Company was out on Picket last
night on the out posts about 4 miles from here and as they were
not allowed any fires they had to keep them selves warm as best
they might   some laid down and slept a short time and waked up
only to find them selves covered with snow   Since I was detailed to
work in the Post Office I have stood no guard duty   I am certainly
glad of it for I think now that my health which is not very [good]
would permit it. Anna you speak of your dislike to boarding house
life there is many a reason for any one to dislike. especially those
that can and do appreciate home life as I think you do. It is
indeed pleasant to recure to the past, to the many happy days
past with the home circle 'ere death with its ever fatal sting entered
our happy circle and took our dearest treasures from us. Who is
there that would forget the past   I would not with all its bitter
grief and all its disappointments and all its joys blended togather
serve only to learn us the value of each friend we possess, to learn
us to go forward with a more earnest purpose in life not to think
of self alone but to try to be useful to others. And who can not
be useful in such a time as this when our country needs every
strong arm that can strike a blow in her defense and we need not
only the strong but we also need the active cooperation of those
that circumstance compel to stay at home which I am sorry to see
is with held by many. And I am afraid that there are men at home
that would willingly see us beaten by the Rebels ere they would
offer any assistance or even speak a word in our favor. But God
forbid that there should be many such in the old 'Sun rise State'.
As for my self I consider it my duty to do all in my power to
help crush this Rebellion. As for others they know what their duty
is as well as I. You ask if I hear from Charlie Additon ever   no
Anna I do not   I wrote to him once but never received an answer   I
was very sorry for I thought a great deal of Charley as a friend   If
Charlie has become disappated as you heard I am very sorry for as
you say he might make a smart likely man. How many a one has
been ruined (by that fatal curse intemperance) whose prospects
in life were bright as they could wish but before they were aware
of it the fatal glass had ruined them. Anna you say that your
letters are uninteresting   pray do not say so again they come like
beems of sunshine on a cloudy day and are eagerly looked for and I
can but feel ashamed to send such letters in return as I do. But
here we are in this wilderness far from a <u>civilized</u> <u>people</u> with
nothing but the daily routine of camp life to pass through   For these

reasons I can but say excuse my uninteresting letters. Please write often. I will now close   Please excuse all mistakes and accept this from Your Ever True Friend & Brother

Abial. H. Edwards
Co K 10th Maine

1. Tattoo is a call to inform men of impending taps so they may get to their quarters. It is usually on bugle, trumpet, or drum and fife.

Stafford Court House.
Stafford County. V=a.
March 6th 1863

Dear Friend Anna

Your kind and welcome letter of the 1st arrived this morning and right glad was I to receive it. My health has been very poor indeed during the last week and it has been a great trial for me to do the slightest duty   But I am in hopes to be better soon. As you say smileing spring has been ushered in leaving cold winter out side by not wholly as we can judge by the cold wind and rains that we have had since then. But this cold will not last long I think for we even now enjoy the pleasure of listning to the Robbin and thrush and a few other birds that never venture so far north as Maine   By the way we have been having some Grand Reviews this last week and the verdict is that the 10th is 2nd to none of the Maine Regiments   the 19th Maine comes next to ours so that General Hooker has allowed more furloughs for our Regiment where as he has stopped many Regts having more furloughs. As you may suppose our boys feel much pleased with their good name. Our Division General A. S. Williams stated that as regards Cleanliness Good behaivior and being well drilled the 10th was the best Reg⊥ in his Division. I hope that we shall continue to keep our good name for a true Soldier thinks as much of the good name of his reg⊥ as he does of his own. Our Colonel G Beal arrived here from Maine to day he has been at on leave of absence for 30 days on account of being sick. You say you have to work 14 hours a day in the mill that must indeed be hard and I hope you will not long have to continue to do so. I think it would now be impossible for me to confine my self in the mill as I did with A K Treadwell. I received a letter from Wm H Mace last week   he did not write much news but still he smeed[1] glad his time of service is so near at end. But still he has done well and I think his heart is in the right place a true patriot.

54

Anna I am ashamed to say I must close my short uninteresting letter which will almost be an insult to return for your long nice letter of last week but I feel very weak (not being able to sit up more than two hours at a time). My will is good to write a long letter but my strength says no how ever if you will please accept this apology this time I am in hopes to be better able to write in a few days. I will write again soon if possible. Please write soon for I shall be so glad to receive your letters

and now Good Night From your Affectionate Friend & Brother

Abial H Edwards

Co K 10th Maine

P.S. Anna Thanks many Thanks for that paper it had many fine stories in it and it helped me to while away a number of hours on my sick bed

Abial

1. Seemed.

Stafford Court House

Stafford Co. VA

Quarters of 10th Maine Regiment

March 17th 1863

Dear Friend

Having a few leisure moments to day, I thought I would improve them in writing to you Tis a cold windy day spring and winter seem to be having a dispute as to who shall rule.

There has been some lively times here lately. A large body of Rebel Cavalry got to the rear of us and went to Fairfax Station and captured one of our Brigadier Generals The youngest one in the service being only 21 years old from there they went to Dumfraies and they were expected to this place and they all got ready here to give them a warm reception. But they did not venture this way. and they got back to their lines in safety our Brigadier with them on the whole it was a disgrace to our army to allow them to get back unmolested. This March wind is fast drying up the mud and a few weeks at farthest will be suitable travelling to give the Rebels another try. Many think that our Reg- will be in another engagement before we leave for home. If it should be our duty [*burned*] them again they will find the 10th ready for them as ever. There is to be a grand review to day of our whole Corps so that I shall not have time to write any more now

From Abial

Stafford Court House
Stafford County
Quarters of 10th Maine Regiment
March 21st 1863

Dear Friend Anna

With the greatest of pleasure I take pen in hand to answer your nice long letter of the 14th which I received last night. Tis' a cold winter day and we are now having another snow storm this being the 2nd day of the storm. We find our thin shelter tents but a poor protection against the bitter cold   I am glad to say Anna that my health is improving althoug I am not well yet   But I am able to attend to the mail and do my duty. Last Thursday our Division was inspected by Major General Hooker   then I saw him for the first time   I was much pleased with his apprearance   He looks as though he was about 50 years old his head is quite white his face inclined to be red rather tall and sits erect upon his saddle. He rides a noble white horse that keeps him far ahead of his aids and body guard and on the whole he has the appearance of being a man that understands his place   He dresses very plainly and if one couldnt see his two stars they would not know that he was so great a man. I could not but watch every movement he made and as he came into the feild the cannon belched forth a salute the numerous bands played a welcome [*burned*] different colors of all Regiments were dipped in his honor. All of which he acknowledged by gracefully raising his hat and bowing his salute. When I thought how much depended on this man how many lives he had in his hands as it were. How much good perchance he might work for his country. I was not disappointed in his appearance. I think that when he moves he will <u>accomplish</u> something   He told our Colonel that he would rather have our Regiment for the next six weeks than any three years Reg- he knew of   this shows that he intends to move soon and that he has work for us. I doubt not that our Reg- will have to do considerable before we start for home. If it is our duty to meet the enimy face to face once more we shall be ready. As for our noble army it <u>never</u> was in a better condition than it is now   the men are just as earnest to meet and conquer as ever they were and as for their not fighting only under such men it is false. The whole army has confidence in Hooker and [*burned*] and all McClellan worshippers included are willing to fight under him and they think that when he does make a move it will be only to lead them to victory.   Let the Copper heads' croak as they will about the army they will find the men are ready and in earnest. Anna I am sitting here in my cold tent the snow sifting in through every crevice

56

with but few personal comforts here but I would not exchange this for the comforts of home purchased by the loss of all manly principal and loss of Patriotism such as these Copperheads enjoy now. I hope the time will come when they will have their just [*burned*] meted out to them   Anna you spoke my mind when you said it was our duty to make all bright and pleasant around us. Far better so even though we felt sad our selves   life at best is full of sorrow and disappointment for us all and tis our duty to make it pleasant as far as it lies in our power. How often have I seen a small party grow morose and cross first by the sullen actions of one of the party where by a few cheerful words and smiles this one might have made all pleasant and so it is we take pattern by those around us   Better be cheerful even if it costs us an effort to be so than cross and sullen   I should liked much to have been there at the Levee[2]   Anna please write me how you enjoyed it   I understand that they are to recruit our Regiment and send it back again   if they do I think that the most of the Regiment will return after a short rest at home. I hope they will for I think that it will be our duty to remain in the service until the Traitors are defeated   I shall be so glad to once more see home and friends   time begins to drag rather heavily to me but a few weeks at farthest if life is spared and we shall see the sun rise State once more

Well Anna I will now close as it is most time for the mail to go out. please write soon and often for time moves slowly of late

> From Your Affectionate
> Friend and Brother
> Abial

1. Copperheads were Peace Democrats, in favor of a negotiated settlement with the Confederacy and bitterly opposed to emancipation.
2. Party.

> Quarters of 10th Maine Regiment
> Stafford Court House
> March 27th 1863

Dear Sister Anna.

With greatest of pleasure I seat my self to answer your kind letter of the 22nd   I was much pleased to hear from you and to hear that you still enjoyed good health

Many thanks for your kind inquiries   my health is improving   all I need now is a little more strength.

There was some prospect of our going to Maryland for the remainder of our time but that has been stoped by General Hooker. In the first class out of the 300 Regiments of this army there is but 11 that stand as first class   ours is one of them and of course he will not spare us now. Our Officers had an order yesterday to send all of their extra baggage to the rear so as to be ready to move at any moment. By that it seems that we have got to go to the front soon. I have been in hopes that it would not be the lot of our reg⊥ to lay away any more of its members in Virginnia but I am afraid that it is not to be so. We are now looking for orders to march every day.

Spring sweet spring has come at last   In the morning we are wakened by the music of birds. The bluebird the Robin the thrush and numerous others fill the air with their melody. And in the evening we have for music the <u>croaking</u> of <u>frogs</u>   The hill side is putting forth its cloak of green and we can once more enjoy our selves in the open air. It is indeed pleasant to watch the glorious sun set in the west These pleasant spring evenings

I am glad you enjoyed your levee. I should liked much to have been there.

All the cases of the small pox that we had in the Reg⊥ has disappeared   it is I think fortunate for us. Anna as it is time for the mail to be sent out I shall have to close   Please accept this short note to day and I will hope to do better next time   Please write soon and often

Please accept this with many kind wishes from
Brother Abial.
Co K 10th Maine.

Quarters of 10th Maine Regiment.
Stafford Court House. Virginnia.
Sunday April 5th

Dear Sister Anna

Your kind and interesting letter of the 30th ult. came at hand yesterday and as usual was glad to hear from you.

We have been having some very changeable weather lately. one day being very fine the next as cold as winter   Last night it commenced to snow and continued to snow until about 10 A.M. to day. Then it commenced to blow and I assure you it is about as disaggreeable as any winter day I ever saw. If this kind of weather continues we shall not be able to move I am afraid until we start for home. By the way General Howard's[1] Head Quarters are here at Stafford Court House. he has taken General Sigels command the 11th Corps. Would that all of our Generals had the interest of their country at heart as much as he has. He is a christian and a soldier [*burned*] as we need. Well Anna I expect that the last of this month will find us on our way Home you say that you shall write to my sister to tie me if she cant keep me at home any other way. I wish you would write to her for she has expressed a wish to me several times that she only knew you. So if you want to keep me in Maine just write to Marcia Edwards Casco, Maine and I dont doubt but what you will find all the help you want. It will give me great pleasure to tell you all I know about Dixie when we get to Lewiston. Now I dont want you to go home by any means until we get there. Will you.

You say Anna that there is two girls that work by the side of you by the name of Crockett. They have got the advantage of me for I dont know of any girls by that name.

Yesterday one of my friends belonging to this Reg. left us to go to [*section burned*] as 1st Lieutenant on the 2nd South Carolina Regiment (Colored). His name is Cassus C. Roberts he is not yet 18 years old he was private in this Regiment. he was one of my nearest friends and I could but feel sad at the thought of parting with him going as he is where new dangers await him never again per chance to see him on earth. But such is life to find friends and just as you learn to appreciate them to have to be seperated from them never to meet again. Anna enclosed you will find a little flower that I found before the snow storm the first I have seen this year. As I am writeing I can hear the Robins chirping as thought [*though*] they were cold Poor little fellows I dont doubt but what they are. I will now close Anna hopping to hear from you soon

Be sure and write and now accept the best wishes of your

Ever True Friend and Brother
Abial H. Edwards.
Co. K 10th Maine Reg.

Anna L. Conant.

1. Maj. Gen. Oliver O. Howard.

Stafford Court House, Va.
Quarters of 10th Maine Regiment
April 17th 1863

Dear Sister Anna

I will write a word to you in the tumult of preparations to march to let you know that we are to leave here We leave here to morrow morning it is now thought to Culpepper which place is now held by Rebel Cavalry. Please write me often Anna and do not think hard of me if you do not hear from me again until we meet   we may go to such a place that it will be impossible to write. If I can I will write to you and let you know where we are. The 'Boys' feel in good spirits and if it should be our duty to meet the foe again they will make their mark   I doubt not but what we shall have work to do within the next few days. Please excuse this short note as I have but little time to spare

Write soon and accept the best wishes of your Good Friend and Brother

Abial H. Edwards.
Co K 10th Main Reg-

Anna L. Conant.

Stafford Court House Virginia
Co K 10th Maine
April 21st 1863

Dear Sister Anna

We are still at our old encampment much to our surprise for we suposed that we should be on the move long ere this. But the last two day we have been having a severe rain storm which has caused the roads to be almost impassible. But we still keep 8 days Rations on hand to be ready for any move. The order came for all of us that is the old members to be discharged keeping the two 3 years company and all the 3 years Recuits here. and they also promise that if any of the old members will reinlist for one year that they will give them 30 days furlough. If our Colonel should remain I think that some would reinlist. And they all say that if government will let us go to Portland as a Regiment that a good part would reinlist after a few weeks visit at home   Ask the Copper heads if that looks like dissatisfaction in the army. By the way we had quite a surprise for our Chaplain this morning. I got up a subscription paper yesterday to buy him a watch and we soon raised 40 dollars and bought him a splendid gold watch and this morning while he was at breakfast the Regiment formed into a square around his tent and gave him an invitation to step out   he came out and then I stept out and presented him the watch in behalf of the Regiment   It was indeed a surprise for he knew not what to say it passed of very pleasantly. Before me is a bunch of May flowers   I will send you one. I wish you could have a whole bunch of them for they are beauties   But a few days more Anna then I hope to be in Lewiston. When I wrote you last I thought that we should move that next day and I should not be able to write you again. I have to be very buisy now as I have to help take care of the Division and Brigade mail as well as Regimental mail   it takes me all afternoon. My health is very good now. Since I wrote to you last I have been called to part with a dear friend and tent mate Alonzo S. Grost   he died very suddenly   we have lived the last 2 years as intimate as brothers he being near the same age as myself   And it seemed so hard so near meeting his widowed mother and twin sister. It seemed harder still his mother lives in Lisbon, Maine   He was wounded at Cedar Mountain and I was the only one that took care of him. He died a good Christian   I can say there is another golden link to bind me nearer that heavenly shore   his remains were sent to his home in Lisbon   It will be some comfort to his poor friends that they can have th[e] privilage of seeing the loved form even in death.

Please excuse this poor letter Anna and if I should not have a chance to write again I shall be in hopes to see you in Lewiston soon and now Goodbye from your sincere Friend and Brother

Abial H. Edwards

PART THREE

Home Leave and Reenlistment,

1863–1864

INTRODUCTION

Edwards and the other men mustered out of the Tenth Maine Regiment were home for over half a year before most of them returned to the war as members of the Twenty-ninth Maine. Congress had passed a conscription act with quotas for each locality. Enlistments counted toward the quotas, so there was a vigorous competition, with cash bounties between the towns. Veterans like Edwards could reenlist in "veteran" regiments under a War Department order of June 25, 1863, and the Maine Adjutant General authorized Colonel George Beal, former commander of the Tenth Maine, to raise one of these veteran regiments. There was a bounty of $400 from the federal government for veterans, an advance bounty of $100 from the Maine state government, and from $200 to $400 from the towns. Advances were paid on January 27, 1864, just before the regiment left Maine.

Edwards was ambivalent about reenlisting. His sister Marcia was ill and needed his care. For a time he worked in a factory producing kerosene lamps, while Anna taught school. Abial's letter of December 16, 1863, indicates Anna and Abial did see each other during this time. But when Captain Nye began to recruit his old Company K, Edwards decided to enlist with his former comrades (Anna appears to have been unhappy with his decision). He reported with Nye on September 17 to Camp Keyes, on the outskirts of Augusta, and traveled around Maine frequently until the company was mustered into federal service on November 13, when they began drilling with new muzzle-loading Springfield rifles. Even after that he was on leave much of the time, until the regiment finally left Maine at the end of January, bound for New Orleans with their old commander Maj.

Gen. Nathaniel P. Banks. There had been rumors that they were headed west to Chattanooga to join Grant, but instead they were to be part of another hard-luck experience with the hapless Banks.

BIBLIOGRAPHIC NOTE

Gould's regimental history, 387–95, discusses the organization of the Twenty-ninth Maine. For the raising of manpower for the Union army, see Fred A. Shannon, *The Organization and Administration of the Union Army, 1861–1865* (2 vols. Cleveland: Arthur H. Clark Co., 1928); Eugene C. Murdock, *One Million Men: The Civil War Draft in the North* (Madison: State Historical Society of Wisconsin, 1971); and James W. Geary, *We Need Men: The Union Draft in the Civil War* (DeKalb: Northern Illinois University Press, 1991).

Casco [Maine] May 14th 1863

Dear Anna

I will write you a short note today to let you know that I am unwell the reason of my not being in Lewiston. I only came home last Saturday and went to see two Sisters which have taken all my time and all this time I have felt rather unwell. One of my Sisters is quite unwell but I am in hopes that she will soon be well. Oh Anna it is real lonesome here and I am in hopes that I shall be able to come over to Lewiston to see you the first of next week   It has been very lonesome indeed to me the most of the time since I have been here

I have not time to write more today Anna as the mail will leave soon but I am in hopes to see you before many days

Affectionately Brother
Abial

Casco May 30th 1863

Dear Anna

I now have the pleasure of answering your <u>kind</u> and <u>so</u> <u>gladly</u> welcomed letter which I got last night after I returned from Lewiston   I went to Lewiston last Sunday and went to your boarding house and was much disappointed to find you had gone home. For I had put great dependence upon seeing you there but I am glad that you are free from the trials of Factory life. I was quite unwell the first week I was at home so that I could not go to Lewiston. Then my sister Marcia was taken ill and is now quite sick. But I hope she will be better soon. Next week I am a going to Woodfores Corner about 1 mile from Portland to stop a few days with Chaplain Knox as he has very urgently requested me to come. We are obliged to stop near here as we are expecting to have our bounty paid us within two weeks. Therefore we shall have to remain here. But after that I think now that I shall have to come up to Canton to see you. I shall be real glad to come to see you Anna. My "School Marm" Sister. Please write Dear Sister soon. As you say one can really enjoy themselves well it is so pleasant. Such beautiful scenes and everything seems so gay. If I should return South I shall not go under four weeks and if I do go I will see you nothing preventing before I leave the State

And now Dear Anna Goodnight
Your Ever True Friend and Brother
Abial
Casco, Maine

Casco June 21st 1863

My Dear Sister Anna

Although I have not heard from you for a long time I thought I would write you a few lines to day to let you know that I am still in Maine. I was in Portland last week we had our bounty paid us last Thursday[1] and now I beleive our Reg- is to be reorganized right away There is great excitement in Portland now. and they will try and send all the troops that they can send right away The 2nd and 10th Maine will be sent back just as soon as possible. Tis a lovely day how much I should like to see you to day Anna but as I can not I shall have to make this short note answer. My Sisters health is improveing slowly and I am in hopes that she will soon be well. And now how do you like school Teaching I came to Casco yesterday and have got to go back to Portland to morrow how long I shall remain there I do not know. I will not write much to day as it has been a long while since I have heard from you. Enclosed you will find a Photograph hopeing it may prove acceptable to you Please let me hear from you soon for I should like to hear from you very much indeed

Please excuse short letter and all mistakes

From Your Affectionate Brother
A H Edwards
Casco Maine

1. This was a bounty of one hundred dollars paid to the men of the Tenth Maine for their previous service, paid on June 18, 1863.

Portland July 24th/63

Dear Anna

I will now take this opportunity to write you a few lines in answer to your kind letter of last weeks which I was much pleased to receive   I should have answered it before but I have been so very buisy that I hardly had time   I have been to work all this week makeing the trimmings for the kerosene lamps. I like it very well indeed.   I like [it] here in the City very much and I think now that I shall remain here this winter if I do not change my mind   I wish that you lived here Anna it would be real pleasant to me. I am acquainted with a good many young men here that belonged to my Regiment but not with any Ladies   By the way I met Sarah Hanscomb on the street the other day   she is now living in the place   you are acquainted with her I beleive. and then again I met Mr Treadwell   He is living in Buxton and came down here to market   he did look <u>rough</u> I assure you   he had an old lame horse and on the whole it was a rough looking team. I saw Bill Mace several times after his Regiment got in   he is the same <u>Villiam</u> that used to work in the Lincoln [Mill]   They have been drafting here for the last two weeks and everything is very quiet   I had <u>7 cousins</u> drafted out of two towns   I feel really honored. The war news I think are really encouraging.[1] They will not reorganize our Reg- now I think until after they get rid of the drafted men which will not probably be for 7 or 8 weeks to come. And as long as my Sister remains sick as she is I dont think I shall return to the army for she is very anxious that I shall remain at home until fall   I am in hopes that you will be in Lewiston soon Anna so that I can come up and see you. I will now close my <u>very</u> uninteresting letter as I doubt not that you tired of it   Please answer soon and oblige your Aff Brother

Abial H. Edwards.

1. The encouraging war news was the victory at Gettysburg and the surrender of Vicksburg on July 4, 1863.

Portland August 20th/63

Dearest Anna

I received your kind and interesting letter last night and now hasten to answer it. As you see I am not yet at Washington or even a Soldier but hope to enlist next week. The reason I have delayed was on account of my sisters poor health but I am glad to say that it is now improving so that I leave without feeling worried about her. I shall stop work here next Monday and we are not called into camp until the 15th of September so that you see I shall have 15 days all to my self. Dindnt we have a fine rain this forenoon Oh how I wish that I had been with you when you visited that mountain but here I have been pretty closely confined for the last few weeks. We have been having some fine Speeches here lately. It is a real treat to listen to them. I have enjoyed my self very much since I have worked here. Portland is a lovely place especially during the summer season no one can help enjoying them selves. I suppose that you are now enjoying your self in real earnest since you have left the confined school House. Do you intend to come to Lewiston this fall. A few of us think of going up to Poland [Maine] one day next week to Camp Meeting as I never attended one yet and I feel quite anxious to go to one. By the way the Prince of Copper Heads is to speak here to morrow night Fernando Wood of New York[1] so you see we have the bitter with the sweet That is a little of Treason even here but it will and must be killed out this fall Oh our home Traitors what are meaner then they even Cain did not have a blacker mark against his name than they will have in future years Now we can see a slight glimmer of that Peace we have so long waited for Fort Sumpter is ours and probably Charleston ere this.[2] and now I am in hopes that a few months will close this dredful war But many will have to fall ere that perhaps my self among the number. But what will it be in comparison to the gain it will bring But I will now close as the bell is pealing out 11 oclock evening so good night Dear Sister Please answer this and direct to Casco

Affectionately your Brother
Abial H. Edwards

Anna S. Conant.

1. Fernando Wood, mayor of New York City and congressman from New York, was a leader of the Peace Democrats.

2. The attack on Fort Sumter was repulsed and the attempt to capture Charleston failed.

Casco Sep- 15th 1863

My Dear Sister Anna

Please pardon me for not answering your kind and interesting letter before for I did not get back to Casco until last night and you may be assured it was eagerly read. Yes Dear Anna I am once more to try the hardships and dangers of war I am agoing to Lewiston Friday and expect to go into Camp at Augusta Saturday or the Monday after.

I would like to see you <u>so</u> <u>much</u> before we leave Maine and <u>I</u> <u>am</u> <u>a</u> <u>going</u> <u>to</u> as I think it will be easy for me to get a furlough for a week and I am acomeing to see you sure   For I should feel rather bad to leave Maine without that privilage. It is a warm pleasant day and my Sister has got her chair by the window where she can look out on the pleasant scene as she is unable to walk out   Oh if you was only here to day how pleasant it would be. You ask how long before we leave for Washington I think not before the last of October if we do then   It seems a good while to me to look ahead and to see my self seperated from the friends so dear to me. Some probably I never shall see again <u>even</u> if <u>I</u> <u>return</u> once more. And I should miss your dear letters so much so please dont change your name right away will you Anna   I suppose that I am selfish in asking such a question for in three years time I expect the most of my young friends will be married and settled in life. While I the self exiled will be many miles from the sun rise state. But being seperated so far apart I have learned only unites the hearts of true friends. Anna when I see you I hope to hear you say that <u>you</u> do not blame me for reenlisting. I saw Charlie Additon last week   had quite a pleasant time with him   he seems to be changed considerable since he left the Lincoln but still the same good hearted Charlie   I hope to see you before many weeks as I have something belonging to you which I wish to hand you my self and I have a good deal to say which I have not time to write now. Please answer this and direct to Casco as the Post Master will send it right on to me. I forgot to tell you Anna that I am still to keep the position of Post Master to the Reg-

I will write no more to day hopeing to see you soon as I want you to write where you are so that if I get a furlough from Augusta that I can see you and now Good Bye

From your True Friend and Brother
Abial. H. Edwards.
Casco. Maine.

Lewiston Sep' 19th 1863

Dear Anna

I thought I would write you a short note to day to let you know where I was. I came up from Portland yesterday and am going to Augusta to [*section burned*] shall hope to see you. As yet I feel it was my duty to enlist although many would look at it in a different way and if I should like to see the end of this war then I shall be able to settle down as a citizen and if I should fall in the defence of all that we hold

67

dear It will be in a good cause. Anna enclosed you will find a small present   Please accept it and wear it for me   may it suit you in size and style   I shall not have time to write any more as the train leaves for Augusta soon   Please write to me right away

[*signature burned*]

Colonel Beal's Veteran Regiment

Augusta Maine

Augusta Oct 8th 1863

Quarters of Col Beal's Reg⊥

Dear Anna

Your kind and welcome missive of the 7th was received yesterday was much pleased to hear from you. By some mistake it was sent to Fort Knox which is the reason that I did not receive it sooner   I have been here all of the time since I wrote to you last with the exception of three days   then I was sent to Portland after some men. But I am in hopes to get a weeks furlough the last of this week to go up to my Sisters and then I shall try and come to see you. As yet the[re] has been nothing said as to our leaving here and I think it a great doubt if we leave here before the Middle of November. The three Companys that we left out South¹ is now transferred to our Reg⊥ and will join us as soon as we leave the state. They are now out west   the last we heard of them they were at Nashville Tenn bound for Chatanouga and many think that we shall join them there. The most of us hope that we shall go there. Where the ablest and bravest of our Generals always head the Western Army on to victory   You say that you would send me your Photograph if you could have one taken provided I wanted it. Certainly Anna I would like it before I leave the state   The one you sent me just before the Cedar Mountain Battle I have carried in my diary with me ever since and it begins to look dim. But I am in hopes to see you before I speak for another. It is rather a dull day for Sunday and only think I have charge of the guard that goes to the city so I have got to go down soon. Will you please excuse this short and uninteresting letter and recollect that my promise to visit you still holds good. But as I am once more under Military control I can not leave just when I <u>would like</u> to

I shall try and go home next Thursday and shall try and come to see you some time during next week

When I go home I shall pass through Lewiston. Please write soon. I would like to hear from you before I went home

Thy loving Brother
Abial H. Edwards
Co K Colonel Beals
Augusta

1. Possibly Companies A, D, and J. Gould's regimental history, p. 308, omits these three in its list of companies mustered out.

Augusta Nov 11th 1863
Quarters of 29th Maine V.V.[1]

Dear Anna

I will write you a note to day to let you know how I am getting along. I was in hopes to get away next Saturday so that you and I could go to Casco but I find that I cant come up then as the orders has come to grant no more passes until after we are mustered into United States service which will be the first of next week   then I will try and get away the first opportunity   I got a letter from my sister last night and she was very anxious to have me come the first opportunity   she said she would be pleased to have us come up to Thanksgiving. I wish we could but am afraid that I could not get away then   But I dont want to fail comeing up before you leave Lewiston. Oh it is so provoking not to have one minute that you can call your own and only think three whole years before I can belong to my self again. But it is a good cause and I ought to be cheerful under it and let the blues take care of themselves. I will try the first possible chance and come to Lewiston. The snow is really here isnt it. It is rather cold camping out here now. But I am in hopes that we shall leave here before many weeks for a warmer climate than this. Please write Anna and let me know when you think of going home. I will now close this short note hopeing to see you soon I remain

Thine
Abial H. Edwards.
Co K 29th M.V.V.
Augusta Maine.

1. Veteran Volunteers.

Camp E. D. Keyes Augusta
December 6th 1863

My Dear Anna

i will try and write you a few lines this cold afternoon to let you know how I am getting along in this cold bleak place. Tis very cold to day and we have to keep pretty near the stove to keep warm. I intended to have gone down to the mill to see you Monday morning but I had to go to Barkers Mills for Capt and did not get back in season. It must be a cold bleake day for you in that boarding house   I have thought of you often to day. It is very lively here now as our Regiment and the 30th is encamped here also the 2nd Maine Cavalry and the Veteran Battery which with the Invalid Corps and General Hospital keeps the City pretty well filled as you can suppose   There is now a prospect of our leaving here within three weeks as our Officers think as our Regiment is nearly full and we are to receive our guns and knapsacks right away.

As yet I think it is not known where our destination will be but it is the general opinion that we shall go to Chatanooga. If so all I will ask for is good health and courage enough to take me through all our hardships & privations. As for the future I can say nothing. If I can return home again when our Country is once more at Pease I think I can settle down and I think I can enjoy the Peace that cost us so much to gain. For I can certainly beleive that we shall yet be victorious   Dear Anna I hope that not many months will elapse before we can meet and talk over the war that was. Till then I must be content with what fortune gives me. I know that I shall feel keenly the seperation from all of you who are so dear to me but it will have to be borne as I hope in the right spirrit. But for me Seperation only strengthens the bond that unites us with the absent ones. Give us your best wishes and love and we will try and prove worthy of the love of the noble ones that we leave behind. Captain Nye is up to Lewiston to day also Lieutenant Bagnall[1] and quite a number of Company K

Please excuse this short and uninteresting letter for it is so cold it costs quite an effort to write to day
Write as soon as you get this

> I remain as ever Thy True Friend
> Coporal A. H. Edwards[2]
> Co K 29th Maine
> Augusta Maine

1. 1st Lt. William Bagnall.
2. Abial has apparently been promoted from private to corporal on reenlistment.

Camp E D Keyes. Augusta. Maine.
December 16th 1863

My Dear Friend

Your kind letter of the 13th arrived in due season and was received with much pleasure though I was sorry that I had forfieted your good will. even for a short time. But again I assure you it was unintentional on my part. But I am sorry that it happened as it did. I suppose ere this you have heard of our being burned out and loosing two of our poor boys. For myself I feel truly thankful that I got out as I did. We lost about every thing we had. The fire caught about 12 at night. I had not been asleep when it was discovered but it spread very rapidly. I got up in my bunk to try and get my things out and got nearly suffocated with smoke   I was the last one to get out I was so stifled with smoke. I found out that the flames was between me and the door and I had to jump out of the window. The flames and smoke followed me instantly   my hand and throat was slightly burned   In that time I heard the poor fellows screaming in their dying struggles   It was dredful   George Libby of Company C a particular friend of mine came over while I was in the burning building and he heard the boys cry "Edwards is in there"   when he heard that he made a rush for the door and they knew that if he did enter the building that he never would come out alive but it took three of them to hold him. But he has nobly proved his friendship for me and I never shall forget it. Anna you said you spent a good part of one day in thinking I was not much of a fellow   I am sorry   <u>Dont judge me</u> by every day outward show for Anna beneath what you call a cold heartless exterior beats a heart as true as ever friend could ask. Some can be easily read while others it takes a long while to find out their dispositions. Be it as it may. <u>Do your duty</u> is my motto even though it may clash with my own personal life. I feel I am doing my duty in serving my country Though many may go for more selfish purposes. I think that it is not so with me. Oh if all the northern men could feel as I do now how quickly would they fly to help in this our time of need. <u>Yes even if they knew that by thus doing they would have to give up all all</u> even life itself. I know not but what my life will have to be given up in this our cause if it should be so. I have <u>only</u> done <u>my duty</u>. I would like to see you again Anna before leaving the state but if you are agoing to return home this week I am afraid I shall not be able to as we are building us new Barracks and we all have to be here. But as you say

71

if we never should meet on earth again may me [we] meet in
Heaven where all seperation all sorrows will be at an end   sometimes
I do feel as though I was doing about my last work on earth
and my earnest wish is to do it in such a way as is right and
that my friends need not be ashamed of me   Three years in the
Battle feild is a long life time to look at and escape uninjured
and for my self I do not expect it. But duty when done in the
right spirrit is sweet even when it costs us a good deal of bodily
suffering

I see by yesterdays papers that I have lost a cousin in the
17th Maine   he was killed in the last battle. He was a noble fellow
and we all shall miss him deeply. Anna I have sent for those large
Photographs of mine shall have them this week and will send you
one. Anna we shall probably leave Maine soon if we do I shall like
to have you still keep up our corrispondence   it would <u>disappoint</u>
<u>me</u> <u>much</u> <u>to</u> <u>have</u> <u>it</u> <u>cease.</u> But I want you to do as you like about it.
If it does not give you any pleasure to keep it up dont continue
it to please me. But hopeing that you feel about it as I do I will
anxiously wait your answer. We now expect Mr. Knox very soon to
come and take the Chaplains position. Lieut Kingsley[1] said he
saw Mr. Treadwell in Lewiston   he was then to start up the Old
Lincoln Mill weave room.

Oh Anna I have got a splendid present by my side it is a neet
pocket Bible given me by our Adjatent[2] who is a great friend of mine.
Tis very cold here now and quite uncomfortable in camp. I <u>do</u> <u>wish</u>
<u>I</u> <u>was</u> <u>comeing</u> <u>to</u> <u>Lewiston</u> <u>this</u> <u>week</u> but shall have to be dis-
appointed. Enclosed you will find a few verses I copied and will send
you as they are just what I should <u>say</u>. I will now close as I doubt
not you will be tired of this long. Dont fail to write just as soon as
you get this

> And now Good Night & God Bless you
> Aff Thy Brother
> Abial H Edwards
> Co K 29 M
> Augusta Maine

"To Anna.
By every feeling that thy heart concealeth
By the strange changes of thy every word will
By the quick glances that thine eye revealeth
Glances that through my very life blood thrill
    <u>Do</u> <u>not</u> <u>forget</u> <u>me.</u>

When silvery music on the night air ringing
Times the quick measure of thy fleet foot's fall
And flattering words to thee bright lips are flinging
Yet thy gay thoughts my earnest tale recall
    Do not forget me.
When in nights musings on thy couch reclining
Thy memory wakens dreams of all the past
Remember one whose hopes round thee are turning
ere sweet sleep chains thee think of me the last
    Do not forget me
If in an hour by chosen friends forsaken
Comes the wild yearning for some kindred heart
Does memory then her slumbering dreams awaken
To tell of ones whose dearest hope thou art
    Do not forget me
By th[e] true friendship we have learned to cherish
Though cruel fate should part my lot from thine
Let not rememberance of the dear past perish
Till life's bright sun grows dim in its decline
    Never forget me"
                   Abial

1. 1st Lt. Albert E. Kingsley.
2. The adjutant was John Gould, who became the regimental historian.

                                Camp E. D. Keyes
                                Quarters of 29th Me.
                                December 28th 1863

Friend Anna

I received your letter tonight and now hasten to answer it. Though at first I will promise you a dry letter as we have no news here of any interest. We are now about ready for the feild probably leave here in a very few weeks. I have not been home yet since I saw you and am afraid that I shall not be able to go again Many thanks for that necktie it is very pretty. It will serve to make me think very often of the giver. Anna I will say now if this correspondence affords you no more pleasure than to help pass away the dark hours of a soldiers life. If you do not derive no more pleasure than that I will not ask you to continue the correspondence any longer. Tis a stormy and disaggreeable night. I have been pretty buisy this week as the Sargaent Major has been gone and I have had to take his place thus I have considerable writeing to do. Please excuse this short note as I have considerable to do before "Tattoo"

Ever Your Friend
Abial H Edwards
Co K 29th Maine

Camp E D Keyes
January 12th 1863[1]

Friend Anna

Your kind letter was received in due season but as I went away the next day after receiving it on a pass, I was unable to answer it until now   I have been away nearly a week got back last night   I was up to see my Sister she was married the 3rd of this month. I had a very pleasant time. I also stoped in Lewiston three days with a friend of mine who is in this Company. I sent that [*illegible*] Photograph up to Lewiston to you and as you had left the young man left it at his house and I have not heard from it since   If I can get it again I will send it to you. We have marching Orders and expect to leave Augusta for Texas or New Orleans next week so you see that we shall have to be pretty buisy to get ready. Our Reg⊥ is full   the 30th is full and as I understand is to go with us. I saw Abbie Eaton while in Lewiston   she is to work in the old Lincoln for Mr Treasewell also "Bill" Mace. We are having some fine weather now which makes it very pleasant for us. As I am on guard to night my letter must necesseraly be short and uninteresting. Please excuse all mistakes and accept this hastily written note

From Your Friend
Abial H. Edwards.
Co K 29th Maine
A Maine

[*This comment written in pencil by Anna*]
Short—I declare. but—not very sweet—Well—just as you like if you like it—

---

1. Apparently Abial had not caught up with the new year. From the date of sister Marcia's wedding, we can place this letter as written in 1864.

Camp E D Keyes
Quarters of 29th Re
January 21st 1864

Friend Anna

Your kind letter was received in due season and I was much pleased to hear from you and to hear you are enjoying your self so finely   May you always be happy is the best wishes of your unworthy friend. We leave Augusta one week from to day the Colonel says   I should be very happy to see you once more but I am afraid that it will be impossible. I will send to Portland for one of those large Photographs for you and Mr Lewis will send it to you. As the Young man that took that other one is very anxious to keep it and I can have one sent you about as soon as you could get that. But I am afraid it will not suit you as I can not have a good Photograph taken   As for your Photograph I would be much pleased to have it if you will only send it to me before next Thursday. I was to a Soldiers Levee last night   it was conducted by Adgt General Hadsdon.[1] We had a splendid time But as I was not acquainted with any of the Ladies I did not enjoy my self as well as many of the rest. Please Write Anna so that I can hear from you once more before I leave the State and Please dont forget me after I leave (Will you. We are kept pretty busy now and dont have much time to be idle which I think is a good thing especally for me for I should feel much worse if I only had nothing to do   Please excuse this careless and poorly written letter Anna as I had just ten minutes to write it in before we went to the City Dont fail to write

From your Friend
Abial H. Edwards
Co K 29th Maine
Augusta Maine

1. Hodsdon was the state adjutant general.

Camp E. D. Keyes
January 29th 1864

Dear Anna

I will write you a short note to night to let you know that we did not leave as soon as we expected to. We leave next Sunday morning go to Portland by Rail Road then take a boat for New Orleans   I dread the voyage but I hope that we shall get along well   Anna please write me a long letter in about a week directing to Co K 29th

Maine Reg' New Orleans. Louisana. Gen Banks Department dont fail to write for I shall be anxious to hear from you. I sent to Mr. Lewis to have him send you one of my large Photographs he will probably send it to you this week. I hope it will suit you. I was much pleased with yours

As I could not get a frame for that Photograph I will send you the money to get one then you can suit your self. Please excuse short note to night as I have a severe head ache. May you ever enjoy the Richist blessings ever bestowed upon mortals. and if we should never meet here again may we meet where friends will never be seperated

> Good Bye Dear Anna
> Good Bye
> Ever Thine
> Abial H. Edwards
> Co K 29th Maine Veteran
> New Orleans Louisana
> Gen Banks Department

PART FOUR

The Red River Campaign,

1864

INTRODUCTION

When Ulysses S. Grant became the commanding general of the Union armies in early 1864, he devised a strategy that would apply simultaneous pressure to many points on the Confederate periphery. The two major Union armies, the Army of the Potomac in Virginia and Sherman's Western Army at Chattanooga, would launch the major assaults against Robert E. Lee and Joseph E. Johnston, but three political generals would also advance to increase the odds.

Nathaniel Banks was one of these political generals, and it was to his Army of the Gulf that Edwards and the Twenty-ninth Maine was sent. Grant had directed Banks to campaign against Mobile, and after that was captured to push north to prevent Confederates in Alabama from reinforcing Johnston in Georgia. Then the administration changed Banks's objective to a move up the Red River in Louisiana to seize cotton and capture Shreveport in order to broaden Union control in that state. The Red River campaign was as much a cotton-hunting expedition for the profit of politicians and generals as it was a military or strategic action. Another Union force pushing south from Little Rock would join Banks before the push on Shreveport. Only after the completion of the Red River campaign would Banks move against Mobile.

The campaign was a failure. The Confederate commander was General Richard Taylor, a wealthy planter of the state and the son of President Zachary Taylor. Earlier he had fought with Stonewall Jackson in the Shenandoah Valley against Banks and he made an accurate assessment of the mettle of his opponent. He attacked the leading elements of Banks's army on April 8 at Sabine Crossroads, thirty-five miles from Shreveport. The Army of the Gulf was routed and driven back, but Edwards and the Twenty-ninth Maine fought well as a rear guard, slowing the Confederate advance. The next day Taylor attacked again, at Pleasant Hill, but this time Banks's army held, with the Twenty-ninth Maine again in the center of the fighting.

Banks decided to withdraw after the troops from Arkansas failed to arrive and the falling Red River threatened to strand the Union gunboats in low water. Wisconsin lumbermen in the army were able to construct wing dams to float the gunboats through the rapids, and the army escaped disaster. It returned to New Orleans in late May, too late to begin the Mobile campaign.

Once again Edwards and his comrades had the hard luck to serve with an incompetent commander. But they demonstrated as a veteran regiment that they were resolute under fire. They did not forget the strange new sights and smells of the Louisiana bayou country and the large number of blacks they encountered for the first time. But they were happy to be done with it.

BIBLIOGRAPHIC NOTE

The standard account of the Red River campaign is Ludwell H. Johnson, *Red River Campaign: Politics and Cotton in the Civil War* (Baltimore: The Johns Hopkins University Press, 1958). Fred Harvey Harrington, *Fighting Politician: Major General N. P. Banks* (Philadelphia: University of Pennsylvania Press, 1948), pp. 140–62, describes Banks's handling of the campaign. Gould's regimental history, pp. 396–462, discusses the role of the Twenty-ninth Maine.

> Algiers opposite New Orleans
> Quarters of 29th Maine Regiment
> Febuary 18th, 1864

Dear Anna

I take this my first opportunity to write to you to let you know that I am getting along finely but am somewhat tired. We got here yesterday   we was on the crowded transport 17 days but fortunetaly I was not sea sick but was troubled considerably with a bad head ache. After we left Portland we did not stop any where but Key West Florida   we stoped there two days to coal up but none of us was allowed on shore as we had two cases of small pox in the Reg[t] and they were afraid of catching it. we got into New Orleans on the 16th at night and yesterday was sent over here and put into an old Iron Foundry which is a very dirty place. We had a fine time in comeing up the Mississippi River I assure you. It is a very low country but th[ere] is some fine looking plantations. Oh Anna I wish you could have some of the fine Oranges that we get here they are ripe now and are very plenty. Algiers is a small city directly opposite New Orleans it is a low dirty place but very few Americans live here mostly negroes dutch etc. etc. There is quite a lot of negro soldiers about here and I think they make a very good soldier But still we have gut that dislike which can not be overcome at once. The nights here so far have been rather cool but I expect that it will be warmer very soon. The 30th Reg⊥ got here last night and are now in the same building with us. It is very hard telling when we shall leave here we may remain here for weeks and may not for but a few days. The prospect is that we shall go to Texas. We had rather a hard time on board of the Transport The sick had to pay ten cents for a small dish of thin gruel and had to pay 25 cents for a can of Ice water and every thing else accordingly you must know how glad we were to be once more on land after being on board of a crowded transport so long. There is no new cases of small pox yet but I am afraid that there will be Anna I hope that that Photograph will suit you. I did not see it and there fore dont know as it was a good one Please let me know when you write Please excuse short note to day dear Anna as I am very tired and dont feel settled yet enough to write a deacent letter I will write again soon and often. I have wrote the first letter to you and now shall have just time to write to my sister before the mail leaves Be sure to write soon and often Dear Anna I will now close this poor apoligy for a letter. Good Bye

Ever Thine
Abial H Edwards
Direct to Co K 29th Maine Reg⊥
New Orleans Louisiana
Gen Banks Department

Franklin on the Byou,
Teche, Louisana
Quarters of 29th Maine Veterans
Febuary 23rd 1864

My Dear Anna

I now take this my first oportunity to answer your kind letter which I received at Algers. It was gladly received and I have read and reread it a great many times. We left Algers the 20th and came as far as Bradhall City by cars then took a boat and came to this place (Franklin) got here on the morning of the 21st   This is a very low country but If the climate agrees with me I think I shall like here. It is very warm here but we have cool nights. The trees are leaved out and the Robins and Mocking birds make music enough. As near as I can find out th[ere] is about 8,000 troops here in our Corps and the Rebel force against us is about 30,000 but they are at Red River which is quite a distance from here. Th[ere] is strong talk of our going to Red River as soon as we get some more troops but I dont think that we shall at present. Th[ere] is quite a lot of Guerrillas about here which are some what troublesome   Anna I have been sitting here and trying to make it seem to me that I am so far from home but I cant and only think for three years. Some times I have thought how much I might have enjoyed my self in Lewiston this summer as you was a going to stop there but it is no use to think any thing about it now   all we must hope for is that this war will be settled before many months. And anyone that has served their Country now will never have cause to be ashamed of it   The[re] is quite a lot of Negro troops here but they are not very near us. As we was comeing here they cheered us loudly as we passed. but our boys kept very still and never returned it. The negros make a neat looking soldier and our Reg⊥ has come to the conclusion that they can and ought to fight as well as white folks but as for cheering them they cant do it. Dear Anna I want you to write often and I will do the best I can to write to you but we have very poor accommodations. We have got the small shelter tents again. My Regards to your Brother & Sister

I will write again soon

Aff Thine
Abial
Co K 29th Maine
New Orleans L-A
Gen Banks Deps

Anna

Franklin on the Byou Leche L-a.
Quarters of 29th Maine Reg⊥
2nd Brigade 1st Division 19th Army
Febuary 28th 1864

Dear Anna

I will write you a letter to day to let you know how we are prospering   It is cool and very pleasant to day. As you see by the head-ing of this letter that we have been Brigated and the prospect now is that we shall have to start on a 200 mile march in a very few weeks by the way of Red River where the Rebel force is now concentrated   I dread the march but shall do the best I can to get through. They are now drawing clothing for us and fitting us out as soon as possible. Our Corps Commander General Franklin[1] was here this morning   He was formarly in the Potomac Army. We have had no mail since we left New Orleans and are now looking very anxiously for one   I think we all should feel better to get a mail   One of our Reg⊥ is to be buried to day[2]   Yesterday morning he went out to chop wood and had a fit falling on his ax and cut of three of his fingers   the Surgeon gave a dose of chloroform and he died right away. Whose turn will it be next   I think that many of us will have to be left out here. I say Anna give me the cold north to live in instead of the south with its ignorant people its loose morals and then the low country, with its snakes lizards Aligators and everything that lives of that land   for my part I dont like here at all on that account. Quite a number of the boys are sick already   coming from such a cold place as Maine was when we left to this hot country has a bad effect on many. But I shall be as careful of my self as possible and trust that my health will still remain good   I will write often Anna but you must not expect long letters as we can find nothing to write about here. I shall want to hear from you often and you need never fear that your cheerful letters will ever make me feel bad   on the contrary It will be real pleasant to me to know that you enjoy your self as well as you do. The more cheerful your letters are the better they will suit me

Please answer soon Ever yours
Abial H Edwards
Co K 29th Maine

1. Maj. Gen. William B. Franklin was the commander of the Nineteenth Corps. The Twenty-ninth Maine was assigned to the First Division, commanded by Brig. Gen. William H. Emory. They arrived at Franklin by steamer from New Orleans.

2. Pvt. Newman A. Savage.

Franklin. Lousiana.
Quarters of 28th M.V.T.M.
March 9th 1864

Darling Anna

I will write you a note to night to let you know how we are getting along   Oh I have got the blues dredfully Anna and I need one of your cheerful letters to make "Richard himself again" Only think have to wait over a month for an answer to the letters we write here. Today we have had several severe Thunder Showers. We have had orders to pack our Dress coats and overcoats and were [wear] only blouses thus showing that we have got a long hard March ahead. The 13th and 14th Maine Regiments came here yesterday and are now in the Brigade with us. By the way when I send you this I will send a you a specimen of the live oak moss. It looks very pretty on the green trees it often hangs in trailing branches of 8 or 10 feet long it is gray and it looks splendid on the trees

I think that our mail has been delayed somewhere on the route but think that we shall yet get it. I dont know Anna but what you will get tired of my writeing so often Oh Anna when this "cruel war is over" what a joyous time it will be. How often I have wanted to have good long chat with you but when I did see you I was contented to hear you talk. I now wish that I could have been more free but if we should ever meet again, I wont be so bashful. May it be ere the three years has passed which is my allotted time in Uncle Sam's service for I that the war must end before that time I will write soon again I <u>must</u> have a letter from you soon or else I will have to <u>come</u> <u>after</u> one. Good Bye Dear Anna

Aff Thy Friend
Abial H Edwards

PS Enclosed is some of the live oak moss   I hope that it will be in good shape when you get it

Thine
Abial

Franklin Lousiana
K 29th Maine Reg-
March 11 1864

Dear Anna

Tis the still quiet hour of eve. I am sitting in my small tent but as is often the case my thoughts are far far from here in the old Pine Tree State. Although thousands of miles seperate us still it is hard for me to realize it. They are very buisy to night prepareing for the march. Our over coats have been sent to the rear our Dress coats also and now all that we have to wear is our blouses   They are giving out Amunition and every thing looks as it used to   a hard march then the Battle feild   every thing looks as it used too but the Recruits can not realize it as we can. Gen Banks is here and is going with us   also about 8,000 Cavalry some Negro troops and the 13th and 15th

Maine Regiments are with us   So you see that we have a Maine Brigade the 30th 29th and 13th & 15th Maine Reg-s   My health is not
very good but I am in hopes that it will be so that I can bear my share
of the burden's laid upon us. About 500 of the 30th Maine is now
sick with the Measels and mumps   we have one man buried to day.[1]
he belonged to Company G. I do hope that we shall get our Mail
before we march far for we must have one soon. I expect that I shall
heer soon of your being in Lewiston once more. If I do I hope you will
enjoy your self Dear Anna better than I do in Lousiana   I will write
no more to night Dear Anna but will enclose lots of Love and Good
Wishes

Aff Thine
Abial H Edwards
K 29th Maine Reg-
New Orleans (via Cairo) La.

as sending them by the way of Cairo they will get here 4 days earlier

Abial

1. Pvt. Sewall W. Mason.

Alexandria La. K29th Me.
March 26th 1864

Dear Anna

Your kind letter of the 3rd was received to day and I was right glad
to hear from you. The last time I wrote to you we were at Franklin.
We left there the 14th and got here yesterday the (25th) Resting one
day having marched in 10 days 185 miles   My feet were blistered
and I am pretty well tired out   When we started this place was held
by the Rebels and we were to capture it but Gen Sherman[1] got in here
a few days before we did and took it. We leave here in a few days to
capture a few places up the River   Th[ere] is 16 Gun boats here to
go with us. Anna I have got a very bad arm having the Erie Sykiles
Inflamation[2] in it but fortunately for me it is my left arm. I cant do
any thing with it but when the Reg⊥ goes again I go with it for I wont
let them put me in a Hospital. below is some verses which speaks my
mind, to A T

> "I have buried in their battle grases
> The days of too stern years
> The earnest days that should have been the spring time
>   of my life
> But regret mars not their coffin with its unavailing tears

I have offered them to Freedom on the alter fires of strife
2nd Tis not enough the call is heard for days that are to come
And other years it may be still the future's hope must give
And I answer to the bugle
To the long roll of the drum
That my country has my service
If it need be while I live"
3rd Yet I would not think of turning
from the comeing march aside
I would not think of halting
with the glory that is past
I will not fail in breasting
The rebellious ebbing tide
As I met its wave's first rising
I will meet them to the last"

It is very warm here now   When I feel better Anna I will write a longer letter but when I sit still so long writing my arm pains me severely. Please excuse pencil for ink is very scarce here just now as th[ere] has been but few supplies brought up since the Rebels left. I will try however and borrow enough of the Captain to back the letter   Dont think that because I write such a short letter that I dont want to write more but to day is the first day that we have had since the march and I feel almost sick

Write soon   when I get able I will tell you all about the country through which we passed   Dont fail to write   I wish I could get your letters sooner Dear Anna

Ever Thine
Abial H Edwards

PS Direct the same as before

1. Maj. Gen. William T. Sherman was not there in person, but one unit of his army was detached to join Banks for a limited time. This was the unit that first occupied Alexandria after the Confederates evacuated it. This corps, commanded by Maj. Gen. A. J. Smith, stirred up bitter resentment in the Twenty-ninth Maine for claiming all of the credit for what little success there was in the Red River campaign.
2. Possibly erysipelas.

Natchitoches, La. K 29th Maine
April 5th 1864

Dear Anna

I will write you a letter to day hopeing that I may have a chance to send it to morrow. I got your letter yesterday just as I sealed the one

I wrote you but did not have time to write you another before the mail left. I was much pleased to hear from you. You ask how I like this country I dont like it at all. From Franklin to Alexandra and 2 days march this side the country is low & sunken. The water being stagnant & very poor. but after we got 2 days march this side the country was a very little hilly and looked much more like Virginia. They raise sugar and cotten here mostly. The Rebels have burned all of the cotten lately so that it would not fall into our hands. Our Gun Boats have gone up the River 8 miles above us and had quite a fight with land Batteries of the Rebels. We could hear them distinctly from here. The rumor now is that we start for there to morrow or next day as the Rebels are strongly fortified. I can truly say that I am ready to undergo all that is in store for me. Much as I dislike the bloody Battle field. I know that it is my duty to be there and do that which I solemnly promised to do. To help conquer all of the enimies of that deer old flag for which so much precious blood has already been spilled. I often think am I better than those who have already given life for their country. NO NO I am not. Oh Anna little did I think a few brief years ago that I was to be in such a great drama of action. How much one has to do now and yet how little one can do. Anna you at home are doing as much as we are out here   your encourageing letters your noble work for the suffering soldiers all all is doing your part nobly. For instance here is Major General Banks who is doing all he can to crush the Rebellion. Also your Humble Brother Abial only a Corporal. But each of us is doing our share. He is useing the many talents God gave him while I am useing the <u>only one</u> that God gave me thus showing that each is doing all that is required of him. Dear Anna probably before you hear from me again we shall have met our foe in Battle. God grant that we may have victory and if I should fall. But never mind we must hope for the best and be ready for any thing that may happen. Darling Anna write often   your letters are perfect treasures and are read a great many times over   If we should not go to morrow and a mail goes out I will write a line more in this   It is very warm to day. and the mocking Birds are singing beautifully. I assure you. Please excuse all imperfections. Write soon

Aff Yours

Abial H. Edwards

K Company 29th Maine

2. Samuel Goodale Edwards, father of Abial Edwards. January 28, 1880, Casco, Maine. Photographer unknown.

3. The Reverend George Knox of Portland, Maine, chaplain of the Tenth
Maine Regiment and later the Twenty-ninth Maine Regiment. Abial
Edwards was fond of Knox, whom he described (Feb. 6, 1863) as "a noble
man and I think a true Christian." Date unknown, photographer Yeaw &
Company, Lawrence, Massachusetts.

4–11. Men of the Tenth Maine Regiment and Twenty-ninth Maine Regiment. Abial Edwards collected over one hundred photographs of his army friends, writing (on May 26, 1865) that "they are bound to me by nearer ties than could have been formed in civil life."

4. George H. Brackett (Tenth Maine Regiment, Company A) of Saco, Maine, 1863. Photographer unknown.

5. Sergeant William E. St. John (Twenty-ninth Maine Commissary) of Portland, Maine, 1863. Photographer A. M. McKenney, Portland.

6. Joseph Chapman (Twenty-ninth Maine Regiment, Company D) of Bethel, Maine. June 13, 1864, Morganzia Landing, Louisiana. Photographer S. Heineman, Louisville.

7. Sergeant A. Guptill (Twenty-ninth Maine Regiment, Company K), 1864. Photographer J. S. Hende, Augusta, Maine.

18. Signature of General Ulysses S. Grant in Abial Edwards's autograph album. Abial obtained it when Grant visited the occupation troops in Florence, South Carolina, in November 1865. Abial's letter to Marcia dated December 1, 1865, relates his account of their meeting. This letter was stored separately from other letters from Abial to Anna, in a box with Abial's autograph album and the gold pen Grant used that day.

Charleston SC

19. Unidentified church in Charleston, South Carolina, 1865. Abial Edwards described it on the back of the photograph as "view of an old Church in Charleston showing the effects of our shells although in the center of the city. . . . All buildings around it had been destroyed." Abial was in Charleston from June 1865 to March or early April 1866, as part of the occupation forces immediately after the war. Photographer H. C. Foster, Charleston.

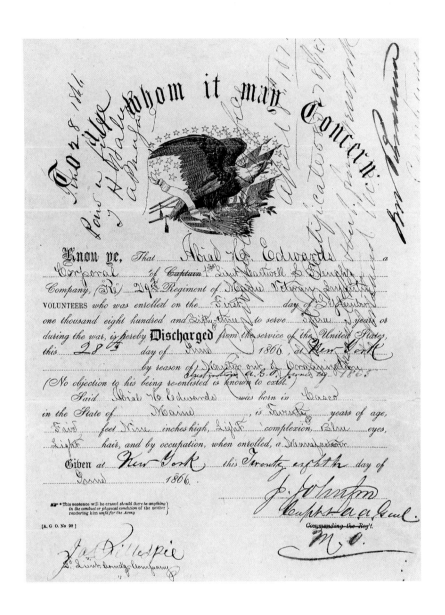

20. Discharge paper of Abial Hall Edwards from the Twenty-ninth Maine Regiment, Company K, on June 28, 1866.

rations for the last 2 days & nights we were completely tired out. Monday we marched back to this place on Red River   the whole army is back here.[4] It is said that the Rebels will follow us up there. but we are agoing to have some more new troops right away then I suppose that we shall try again   Yesterday the[re] was a mail came for us but I got no letter from you   was sorry for it but I got a letter from My Sister which did me heaps of good. Oh Anna I am so tired & weary   Thank God you do not know the trials of the Battle Feild. The hard marches and all the trials of a soldiers life but we are not dis heartened yet. We shall yet see Victory though perchance I may never live to see it. But there is rest for the weary beyond all this trouble. A land where war and its horrors never come. Several of my friends was wounded in the Reg-. I am so tired Anna that you must excuse my poor letter   soon I will write again and try and do better. Write soon and often Dear Anna. Dont fail to. I will write as often as possible.

> From your Aff Friend & Brother
> Abial H. Edwards
> K 29th Maine

1. The Battle of Sabine Crossroads (the Battle of Mansfield, to the Confederates) on April 8 was, as Edwards describes it, the scene of savage fighting in which the Twenty-ninth Maine fought bravely as a reserve to check the Confederate advance.

2. Again, at the Battle of Pleasant Hill on the following day, the Twenty-ninth Maine acquitted itself well in stopping the Confederate tide. According to Gould, the best estimate is that the Twenty-ninth Maine suffered casualties of 40 killed, wounded, and taken prisoner out of 534 engaged. No one from Company K was killed.

3. Corp. Albert N. Dunn.

4. "Back here" is Grand Encore, near Natchitoches.

> Maganzia[1] Landing,
> Mississippi River, La
> Head Quarters 1st Brigade 1st Div
> 19th Corps
> May 24th 1864

My Dear Friend

After a long silence I will now endeavor to write you a letter to let you know how we have got along for the last few days. Friday 13th we left Alexandria in the morning   just as we left the Rebels came up and shelled our Gun Boats. Alexandria was set on fire (supposed to have been done by the negroes) and all of the buildings were burned the Rebel Pickets troubled our advance some. got into camp at 1 at night Sat 14th In the morning we found where the Revels had captured our mail going up to us and also one the we had sent away The ground was strewed with Envelops I found part of a letter that I had wrote to my Sister. I wrote to you about the same time. Today the Rebels fired into our Hospital Boat and killed 2 & wounded several They did this even when the Hospital Flag was flying. (May the[y] have their reward) To day I and a squad of men went with the Brigad Teams as guard between the road & River is a Levy built up of dirt six feet high and as it was much cooler we walked on it. All at once the Rebels fired a volley into our squad but fortunately hurt no one we got down from the levy and walked by the side of it as it afforded us considerable protection. They kept a fireing to us for about 1 mile all the time some times the bullits just skipping our heads. Once th[ere] was some trees just between us and the river and I thought they would not see us so I got up on to the Levy but in a second three shots was fired at me and I just steped down they kept pretty well out of our sight and we had to fire at them at random. Heavy skirmishing in our front to day. Reached our camp ground at 12 at night Sunday 15th Fighting in our rear and front to day marched 10 miles and encamped near Knoxville 2 1/2 miles from Fort De Russey. The 19th & 13th Corps in front then comes the wagon train which is 19 miles long then the 16th & 17th Corps in the rear of the Train to guard that as Rebels are in rear & front of us Monday 16th a Battle fought near Knoxville Co K was sent out as skirmishers and drove the Rebels and marched 18 miles Tuesday 17th hard fighting in our rear to day. Rebels attached [attacked] our Train & Cattle but we drove them of We marched to Simsport on the Atchafalaya River. After we got into camp the Rebels came and fired at us from accross a small Byou. We drove them of however and the killed one man and wounded several Wends 18th a hard Battle[2] fought 2 miles from here by the 16 & 17 Corps commanded by the <u>Fighting</u> General A J Smith Fought all day the wounded came in in the afternoon by hundreds at night the[re] was 100 men working all night digging graves and burrying the dead that died on the boats of their wounds. Thurs 19th we crossed the River and marched about 4 miles. Heavy skirmishing in our rear about 300 Rebel prisoners brought in 20th We laid in camp until 6 P.M. and marched until 6 Saturday morning Rested until 9 Saturday morning then we marched to the Mississippi River 15 miles when we got there we found a mail for us I got 11 letters & 9 [*burned*] I was much pleased to get 2 letters from you one of the

25th and one of the 15th of April   I hope now we shall get our mail more regular. We are all tired out and the Reg- is very sickly   some one dies about every day and once or twice we have had 4 die in one day   We are now waiting further orders   We shall probably leave here in a very few days. I am still at Brigade Head Quarters and like much. Please write often Anna. After I get rested I will write a better letter but now I am so weary. Dont fail to write

Aff Thy Friend
A H Edwards
Co K 29th Maine

many thanks for those may flowers   my favorites.
Enclosed is a rose from the Battle Feild   2 1 the 28th of this month I am growing old

1. Morganzia.
2. This was a bloody rear guard action.

PART FIVE

With Sheridan in the Valley,

1864–1865

INTRODUCTION

After an uneventful voyage north from New Orleans, the Twenty-ninth Maine arrived at the Potomac on July 13, in the immediate aftermath of Confederate General Jubal A. Early's raid to the gates of Washington. As soon as they landed they were marched off to join in pursuit of Early. After several days at an exhausting pace, they were back in the Shenandoah Valley, familiar to Edwards and the Tenth Maine veterans as the locale of defeats in 1862.

Grant determined to put an end to the threat of Early and to the Confederates' use of the valley as an avenue of invasion and a granary for Lee's army. To command the Union troops in the valley he appointed the dynamic but diminutive Maj. Gen. Philip Sheridan from the western army. His newly created Army of the Shenandoah included two divisions of veterans of the Red River campaign. Grant ordered Sheridan to go after Early "and follow him to the death."

Sheridan started slowly, aware of the long series of Union defeats in the valley and the fact that Early had been reinforced by Lee. Then, in mid-September, Sheridan learned that Lee had recalled one of these divisions, and he decided to attack. On September 19 he struck the Confederates at Winchester and sent them flying. Early, with heavy losses, retreated south to Fisher's Hill near Strasburg. Here on September 22 Sheridan attacked again, broke Early's lines, and sent the Confederates into a sixty-mile flight to the south. In relative safety Early was able to pause and recover.

The Twenty-ninth Maine at Winchester fought on the right, which was not nearly as hard-pressed as the left wing of the brigade, and under good cover, so its casualties were light: four killed and twenty-two wounded, none from Company K. But one of those killed was Major William Knowlton, the regimental commander who had replaced Beal when he was promoted to brigadier general and given command of the brigade. At Fisher's Hill, the Twenty-ninth Maine fought on the periphery and was fortunate to have no one killed and only four wounded.

With Early's threat removed, Sheridan then proceeded to devastate the Shenandoah Valley so it would no longer feed Lee's army. Crops and barns and mills were destroyed, and livestock killed or driven off. There was some harassment from Confederate bushwackers and guerrillas but little Confederate army presence.

Lee and Early, however, had decided to make another try at holding the valley. Aware that Early had been reinforced, Sheridan left his army in camps near Cedar Creek, about fifteen miles south of Winchester, and went to Washington to confer with Grant about the next move. Early then made a surprise attack. After moving his troops silently into position through very rugged terrain, he threw them at the Union camps along Cedar Creek at dawn on October 19. The surprise was complete. The Army of the Shenandoah was routed and fled four miles down the valley.

By mid-morning, the Confederates believed that they had won. But part of the Union line had held, and Sheridan had arrived back from Washington. Racing to the battlefield, he rallied the stragglers, and they followed him back to the front. It was, says James McPherson, "the most notable example of personal battlefield leadership in the war" (*Battle Cry of Freedom,* 779). Sheridan reorganized his army and that afternoon he counterattacked. Early was sent reeling to the south, his army disintegrating as it fled.

Sheridan had won a decisive victory at Cedar Creek and the Twenty-ninth Maine had been in the thick of it. Major George H. Nye was now in command of the regiment, promoted from the rank of captain on October 18, 1864. It had, with the rest of the army, been surprised by the Confederate attack in the dawn mists, but managed to retire in good order and stop and fight three times before the word came of Sheridan's arrival. Edwards and his regiment were part of the counterattack, which began, for them, about four in the afternoon, fighting on the extreme right. By dusk they had recovered the camps they lost in the morning, but at high cost. Their casualties were twenty-nine killed and ninety-eight wounded, the heaviest losses of the war for the Twenty-ninth Maine, but less than the Tenth Maine had sustained at Cedar Mountain in 1862.

Cedar Creek was the last major fighting of the war for the Twenty-ninth Maine. Sheridan and many of his troops went to join Grant around Petersburg and Richmond, but Edwards and his regiment remained with the reduced Army of the Shenandoah, now commanded by Major General William H. Emory, to patrol the northern end of the valley. They located at "Camp Sheridan" near Stevenson's Depot, and Edwards was appointed postmaster for the brigade. Here they spent a fairly quiet time, interrupted by a twenty-day furlough to Maine at the end of 1864, until the war ended.

BIBLIOGRAPHIC NOTE

The standard account of Sheridan's campaign in the Shenandoah Valley is Jeffrey D. Wert, *From Winchester to Cedar Creek: The Shenandoah Campaign of 1864* (Carlisle, Pa.: South Mountain Press, 1987). It may be supplemented by the earlier Edward J. Stackpole, *Sheridan in the Shenandoah* (Harrisburg, Pa.: The Stackpole Co., 1961). For the part played by the Twenty-ninth Maine, see Gould's regimental history, pp. 463–572.

> In camp Near Frederick City, M = d.
> HeadQuarters 1st Brig 1st Div
> 19th Comp
> August 2nd/64

My Dear Sister [Marcia]

I wrote you a few hasty lines night before last as we expected to leave yesterday but we did not leave as the Rebels have left Penn and th[ere] has been no orders as yet for us to leave to day. I was pretty sick yesterday so that I did not sit up much but this morning I feel better. Our Reg⊥ now numbers only 220 men for duty. My Company only 20 men and not a commissioned officer all the rest being in Hospital   To let you know what a time we have had I will commence to the time we left Georgetown and let you judge for your self. July 26th we left Georgetown at noon   we marched through Tanlytown and 4 miles beyond Rockville got there at 2 Oclock on the morning   marched 20 miles of [on] 27th   we stoped here 3 hours and started at 5 a.m 27th and marched through Hyattstown & encamped within 4 miles of the B & O Rail Road   marched 22 miles Thursday 28th we left camp at 6 A.M. crossed the Monocaly¹ River & the B & O R. R. marched through Frederick and encamped near Jeffersonville   got into camp at 2 Friday morning having marched about 28 miles   we left again at 6 Friday 29th they being kind enough to give us 4 hours rest   we marched through Knoxville crossed Potomac and marched to Halltown 4 miles beyond a distance of 24 miles, Sat 30th Left camp at 3. P.M. on the road all night   Sunday 31st we got into Frederick and 3 miles beyond in the 2 days marching about 38 miles. So you can see just how much rest they gave us. Do you wonder that we are all tired out. Capt Nye is in Hospital also Lieut Bagnall. Th[ere] was only 2 Brigards of our Corps here the rest being down with Butler.² They had a dredful fight down there. One Reg�)⎻ in our Corps lost 100 men   The 30 was not in it as they were on Picket. The Corps has now got back here   It got up yesterday. Enclosed you will find a piece of bark taken from the tree John Brown was hung on³   It is a Bonifide peice   when we were at Halltown we was within 2 miles of it   one of our Cavalry men that was out there got it gave it to me. I think that we shall have to leave here this afternoon sure so will have to draw my letter to a close

Write often

> Aff Thy Brother
> Abial
> Love to All
> Phebe Ester & all

1. Monocacy.
2. Maj. Gen. Benjamin F. Butler, who was campaigning on the James River.
3. Abolitionist John Brown was executed at Charles Town on December 2, 1859, for his raid on the U.S. arsenal at Harpers Ferry. He was hanged on a gallows, not a tree.

> Head Quarters 1st Brigade 1st Div
> 19th Corps Hall Town. V=a.
> August 9th 1864

My Dear Friend Anna

Your kind letter of July 5th was received to day and I take great pleasure in answering it. I feel very guilty in not writing to you before but when I give you my reasons for not writeing I hope you will pardon me   I was very unwell at Morganzia for a long time so much so that I did no duty. The 3rd of July we left Morganzia for New Orleans and spent the 4th there   On the 5th we started for Washington, D.C.   Got there the 11th of July and was amediately started for the retreating Rebels   Since then we have constantly on the March through Virginnia & Maryland. Not getting any mail hardly being so tired that when we did stop we did not feel like writing. And therefore our Friends have been neglected. My health has been very poor and it has been a great task for me to do my duty   The-Surgeon says my heart is diseased but for a day or two past I feel better. If the duty had not been light I could not have got along. The hard marches have cut down our Reg⊥ a great deal. In my Company th[ere] is only 23 Muskets. Capt. Nye is sick in Hospital. Lieut Kingsley[1] is dissmissed from service and Lieut Bagnall[2] is dead   The Company is commanded by Lieut French[3] of Camp H   We are now 4 miles from Harpers Ferry. Came here day before yesterday. The enimy is in front of us in Heavy force   rumor says their Pickets is only 4 miles from here and yesterday we had 20 Pickets wounded. We shall probably move forward to morrow   if so it is expected that we shall have a hard fought Battle. All I will ask for is good health. I dread the thoughts of a Hospital. Now Anna I want you to write often dont let us have so long a silence as we have had. I will promise to do better my self. I have missed your letters sadly. I will write often. I have had but very few letters lately and it makes time drag heavily I assure you. Hopeing to hear from you very soon I will now close

> Ever your true Friend
> Corpl Abial H Edwards
> Direct to
> Head Quarters 1st Brigade
> 1st Div 19th Corps
> Via Washington DC

1. Albert Emerson Kingsley was dismissed on June 2, 1864, due to injury at Cedar Creek, but was reinstated when a special order of the War Dept. requiring dismissal was revoked in January 1859.
2. William Bagnall died in Louisiana of gastritis on July 10, 1864.
3. Hartwell S. French.

> Near Middleton
> Shenandoah Valley, Va.
> Head Quarters 1st Brig 1st Div
> 19th Corps
> August 15th 1864

My Dear Friend.

I will write a few lines to day hopeing it may prove acceptable. We left Hall Town the day after I wrote to you passing Through Charleston [Charles Town] & Berryville. We were 3 days comeing to this place. as the Rebels were in front of us and our Cavalry was fighting them every day. They were finaly drove back to this place. and their line now rests on the opposite side of the Shenandoah River 1 mile from here where they have their Pickets stationed also their Batteries. The Pickets have some fighting every day here which can plainly be heard here at camp   I hardly know what we are waiting for now un-less the Rebels have a very heavy force here. We have been here 2 days and we expected to follow them up the first day we came here. By the way I saw in the Lewiston Journal that Wm H Mace of the 32nd Maine was mortally wounded & died at City Point [Virginia]. Pour William   He was always deeply interested in our Countrys cause   He has done his duty nobly offering up all in his path of duty and now may he meet with his just reward. Lieut Bagnall of my Com-pany died at New Orleans   He has a family living in Lewiston   We have lost a good many of our best men this summer. Our sever cam-paign in Lousiana then comeing here and entering upon another al-most as severe in hardships is telling upon all of us. The Guerrillas are very troublesome in our rear   Day before yesterday they captured quite a number of our teams and burned them   They were loaded with rations and were comeing to us when captured.

Our Cavalry Captured a Rebel spy Saturday   he came into our camp selling stationary stamps etc and was recognized by a Cavalry Adj⊥ who had seen him and talked with him while he (the Adj⊥) was prisoner in Richmond. Our Cavalry took the spy & hung him as soon as his guilt was proved. I anticipate some hot work here soon for we have a large army and we are commanded by a General well known for his success (General Sheridan) in all his undertakeings   For my part I dont care who commands us if he will only lead us on to vic-tory. For I am tired of the war heartily tired of it. Oh how I long for that Peace we once had   Dont think because I say this Anna that I am turning Coppery   Oh no I want it setteled right & just   Well I will now close as I have some work to do.

Aff Thine
Abial H. Edwards.

Head Quarters 1st Brig 1st Div.
19th Corps Hall Town, Va
August 24th 1864

My Dear Friend Anna

Your kind letter of Aug 18th was just received and I was much pleased to hear from you I assure you. I beleive we was down the valley at the time I wrote to you last. Well Gen Sheridan found the Rebels to strong to attack and as they had got reenforcements he thought it best to fall back to this place which was done   we passed through Winchester & Charlestown the Rebels following us very closely skirmishing every day. We have now been here 3 days th[ere] is skirmishing at our front every day. 1 mile out in plain sight   Now they are ha[rd] cannonading on both sides & Infantry Picket fighting which makes it lively I assure you   I have been watching the Pickets for the last 2 hours but was just called to get the Brigade Mail and to the more pleasant duty of reading your letter. The Rebels force here is 55,000 our not quite as much I should judge. I think we shall have a Battle here before they leave but we have a very strong position which they <u>cannot</u> <u>take</u> Try as they may. My health now is very good   You dont know how pleased I was to get your letter for I have missed them saddly but as you say dont let another such long silence ensue. You ask why was Lieut Kingsley Dissmissed. It was through the meanness of some officers at New Orleans   But it did them no good for he has been reenstated and joined us yesterday and you may be sure that we was glad to meet him again. I am sorry that you had such a lonely time this summer but hope that you will make it up this comeing winter. 50 Rebels prisoners was just carried by that was captured this afternoon

Oh Anna I shall be so glad when this war is over   I see the dredful effects of it more & more every day   would that we could settle it this summer but thank God old Maine has not yet seen its effects if they have felt it in a measure   I feel thankful that my state is so far from this war. I lost a Dear Cousin last week before Petersburg   How sad so many falling so little gained. Would that my mind was comprehensive enough to see the good. But still I think that if Mobil is captured & Atlanta that little good will accrue from it. Well I must now close as I have got to go out to Harpers Ferry to night. Dont fail to write soon Anna. Time will fly much faster than it does now to get letters from you.

Aff Your True Friend
Abial. H. Edwards.

In Camp Hall Town Virginnia
Head Quarters 1st Brig 1st Div
19th Corps
August 25th 1864

My Dear Friend

I will improve this evening in writing a few lines to you hopeing they may prove acceptable. To day quite a hard fight was fought up on our right. About 200 of our wounded was brought in and sent to Harpers Ferry. We still have Picket fighting in front of us day and night and we have become so used to it that we hardly notice it. It seems to me a cruel practice for the Pickets to fire at each other so when it does neither side any good   We are very buisy now in throwing up breast works & digging rifle pits so that I think that it will give them a hard time for them to take these heights   While we was down the valley we was troubled a good deal by the Guerrillas in the rear of our army   once they captured and burned 60 of our Supply Teams which was comeing out to us with rations and last saturday 2 of the 29th boys went out a short distance from the Reg^{t} and was captured by the Rebels. One of them got away from the Guerrillas after he gave up his gold watch & pistol but they carried away the other man   his name was John Kincaid of Lewiston. The night before that Col Davises cook went out to a hous about 1 quarter of a mile from camp and the woman told him to come out the next morning and she would sell him some bread & butter for the Officers   He went out as she told him and bought the bread and started for camp   he had gone but a short distance before 3 Guerrillas overtook him and told him to serrender   he refused to do so when one drew his sabre and run it through his breast and another shot him dead with his revolver   one of our boys saw it a short distance of came into camp and told of it   when they went out and got his body it was horribly mangled such was the murder of an unarmed soldier. Gen Emary[1] sent out a guard to this womans house and searched it and they found the 3 men in the cellar and $30,000 dollars in US money which they had most likely robbed our soldiers of. I have not yet heard what he has done with the men   Th[ey] ought to be hung. You asked me Anna if I went to the Hospital while I was sick. No I did not if I had I dont think I should have got up again. I staid in camp and had good care where it was quiet and got along much better than I expected. And you cant imagine how glad we were to get up here in V.A. It was so hot and unhealthy that I was heartily sick of the place   here the climate is almost like that of Maine   you have of course seen about Lieut Kingsley being at home   well he has been reenstated and is now with us commanding the company

I see that they still have hard fighting in Grants Army. How sad it seems to take a Maine Paper and read the long list of killed & wounded every week of Maine's sons. It seems to me that Maine has suffered more according to her population than any other state in the Union. I had a friend who served in the 10th Maine with me   He was about my age   While in the 10th his Farther died leaving only him & his Mother so he was an only child   he went home with us. After I enlisted he came to Augusta to see me. Ever patriotic he was anxious to join us in the 29th but the prayers of his widowed Mother prevailed and he consented to remain at home with her. But in the month of June when every one saw the need of troops he told his Mother he thought it his duty to enlist again   his Mother at last consented (God alone knows with what struggles) and he enlisted in the 2nd N H Cavalry. They went amediately to the front at Petersburg and the first time they went on Picket Poor George was killed   He was Sargaent and led a squad of men into a peice of woods where the Rebel lay concealed. He was shot from his horse and the horse went back to the company riderless and fell dead in the place that belonged to him. They did not get Georgies body   Thus perished one of my best friends a faithful son true to his country. A gifted scholer. Every thing in life looked bright to him. He has given up all. You cannot imagine how I miss his cheerful letters. At the same fight I had a cousin killed   it seemed hard very hard to think how little has been gained through so much sacrafice. Can it be that we deserve all this   Friend after Friend has gone before but they will never be forgotten while life lasts   How anxious I am to hear of the fall of Mobile & Atlanta if they should fall I think it would look more encourageing to to all. And Petersburg to I want to hear of the down fall of that place   It is said that it is always darkest just before day and I hope our next news will verify the old adage. I am writing by candle light it is now 10 in the evening and late as it is I can hear Picket fireing quite often   Many think that we shall be attacked here soon   if so I feel that the Rebels will get worsted. General Sheridan commands this army and he has the name of being a smart officer   Capt Nye has gone home sick   I under stand that he is trying for promotion in some new Regiment. I hope he will succeed. Our 2nd Lieut Wm Bagnall of Lewiston is dead and Alpheus L Green our Sergaent Major has been appointed 2nd Lieut   he is from Portland and was in the 10th with us before   I am afraid that my letter will be uninteresting to you Anna but I thought I must write some thing to you if it was not so interesting   My letters seem to be few & far between from Maine lately. and I want to hear from you often. I think we shall remain at this place for a few days if not weeks. I hope so for we need the rest sadly. I will now close by saying write often and I will do the same. and now Good Bye

Ever Thy Friend
Abial H Edwards.
direct K 29th 1st B 1st D 19th C
Via Washington D. C.

1. Maj. Gen. William H. Emory.

> In camp near Berryville, Virginnia.
> Head Quarters 1st Brig 1st Division
> 19th Corps
> Sep⌐ 6th 1864

My Dear Friend Anna

Having a few leisure moments to day I thought I could improve them in no better way than in writeing to you. We got marching orders Friday night and Saturday morning we left camp at day light and crossed over into the Berryville Pike and marched to within 2 miles of Berryville There we met the Rebels and they had quite a fight our 2nd Division was engaged also a part of the 8th & 6th Corps They fought about 2 hours until dark stoped the Bloody work. we laid in line of Battle all night and it rained very hard so we passed a very disaggreeable night Sunday morning the Rebels did not advance and our troops commenced entrenching Their Pickets advanced their lines to within sight of the 29th They were fighting all the afternoon. We had orders for every thing to be ready for a Battle yesterday (Monday) but the Rebels did not advance. and as General Beal was General Officer of the day he had orders to take the 47th Reg⌐ out and see if the Rebels were still in force, as one of his Orderlys was sick and I asked Adj⌐ Gould if I could go out with him as Orderly He said I could if I wished. I took the Orderly's Horse (which was a white one) and went out with him. Gen Beal 3 of his aids 3 of us Orderly's was all mounted we started out and when we got near the woods where the Rebel sharp shooters were we was rideing along when a bullet came whistling along over the General's head and just skiped by my head so near that I felt the wind it was followed by 2 more the General turned around and laughed said he thought my white horse caused the Rebels to pay us particular attention. He ordered the 47th Reg⌐ to advance into the woods which they did. The bullets began to come so thick that we was obliged to dismount. We remained out there from 9 A.M. until 2 P.M. all the time being under fire. General Beal was in the thickest of it all the time. Every time we got out in sight it seemed as though a dozen Rebs had as many bullets ready for us some times the bullets sounded like wasps whistling around as Lieut Edely on Gen Beals staff was ordered to go accross a small cleared place twords the Rebels to tell the Lieut of the skirmisers to retire he told me to take his horse and throwing of his coat he started on the run. The bullets flew around him like so many hail stones and when he came back they fired at him the same but fortunately not one hit him. He came back laughing & said that was a gauntlet he didnt care to run every day. At 2 P.M. we had orders to retire as we had found the Rebels there in force. When I came back the Adj⊥ said I deserved a good dinner for volunteering to go into such a place. so he gave me some nice biscuits for dinner. The boys had quite a laugh over it   They said they thought my first days trial as orderly was rather rough. Today it is raining very hard and it is very disaggreeable I think we shall advance in a day or two. I am in hopes that we shall get a mail before we start ahead. The Rebels have been reenforced very lately also their Cavalry has had new horses so when we do meet them in a general engagement it will be a hard fight. I will write no more to day For I am in hopes that I shall get a letter from you before I have a chance to send this

Ever Your True Friend
Abial

Camp near Berryville. Va
Sept 14th 1864

My Dear Friend Anna

Your thrice welcome letter of the 4th I got safely last night and I was much pleased to hear from you. I assure you I am very sorry to hear that you are unwell   hope this will find you better. It has been very quiet since I wrote to you last and we are enjoying a rest which we so much needed   This morning the 2nd Division of the 6th Corps went out on a reconoisance and by the heavy boom of Artillary in the direction of Bunker's Hill It shows that they have found the Rebels you ask me what I think of the nomination of McLellam[1] If he accepts his nomination with such surporters as Vollendigham[2] and other Copperheads I shall consider him one of their mean tribe. But I think he is too much of a man to be mixed in with them. I think there is but two parties now. Unionists & Dis Unionists and I think as much of a war Democrat as I do of a Lincoln man. But for my part I want to see Lincoln reelected. The Chicago Platform[3] wants us to stop hostilities where they are. What stop now throw away Shermans victories Grants victories, Farraguts[4] & Grangers[5] victories. Give the Rebels an armistic let them recruit their wasting armies let them have what they want. Such I take as the wish of this Chicago Platform when we do   This [thus] we disgrace the memory of our fallin brothers   no much as I desire Peace I Had rather remain here and if it need be lay down my life before we give up one iota of the victories we have gained to the Rebel hords. The name of such men as Vallandigham will yet be as much of a disgrace as the name of Arnold now is. For my part I dont think McLellam

will accept such a nomination   if he does it will not be with such
supporters as the Convention has but time will show for us   Let our
armies be recruited and I think another summer will see this strife
closed and our armies victorious. not a beaten disgraced army as the
Chicago convention would have us. But time will decide all things for
us. But I think even is McL- is elected that he will be just and do
what is right for I consider him far from a Traitor   We are now having some very cool weather. Lately the Guerrillas have troubled us
some what. They have captured some of our Reg⊥ that has been out
forageing. I will close this as I think I shall have a chance to write
again before the mail goes out. So dont accept this as a letter.

From Your Ever True Friend
Abial H Edwards

[written upside down at the top of the first page]
Anna I know I should enjoy a quiet talk with you very much hope
many months will not pass ere I can have that privalage

Abial

1. Maj. Gen. George B. McClellan was the Democratic nominee for President in
1864.
2. Clement L. Vallandigham of Ohio was the leading Peace Democrat or Cop-
perhead.
3. The Democratic national convention at Chicago adopted a plank in the platform calling for an armistice and negotiations for peace.
4. Rear Adm. David G. Farragut, who captured Mobile, Alabama, on Aug. 5,
1864.
5. Maj. Gen. Gordon Granger, who led the land assault on Mobile.

Fishers Hill, Near Strausburg. Va.
october 10th 1864

My Dear Friend Anna

Your kind letter was received in due season but oweing to our moving right away I could not answer it before this time   We left Harrissonburg the 7th and got here the 9th   a force of Rebels followed us
closely and we was skirmishing with them all the march   Saturday
they got so near to our signal Corps on Fishers Hill as to fire into
it   Co K & D 29th Maine was ordered up to drive them away which
they did in fine style not haveing a man injured   yesterday Sunday
the[re] was quite a Battle fought here lasted nearly all day   Resulted
in the rout of the Rebels and we captured 11 Cannon 45 wagons 300
Johnnies & all of their amunition   this makes the 3rd great victory
that Sheriden has had in this valley. The fighting on our side was

mostly done by Torberts' Cavalry. It is <u>very very</u> cold here now too cold to be comfortable. Well Anna you are back to Lewiston are you. I certainly hope that you will enjoy your self this winter   <u>Perhaps</u> I may get a furlough this winter and come home   if I do I shall of course call at Lewiston. You ask if I have heard from my Sister and her husband   I have he is still very sick, dangerously so. He was drafted out   they will have to wait a long while before he will be able to go. I have been thinking how bad I should feel to be drafted and be obliged to leave my home against my will. But it has to be done and I feel thankful that I dont have to be one of them   It has been <u>very</u> cold here for the last few days and we have suffered considerably as we left our overcoats in La [Louisiana] and have had none since. Sunday last during the battle I was troubled with the chills very bad and it was very cold   we was in the woods on the North side of Fishers Hill and you may be sure I suffered. I dread this winter much. Many think that we shall go (a part of this army) to reenforce Gen Grant. I hope that it wont be our lot to go for I think that we need a few weeks rest very bad. A new company has joined the 29th from Lewiston called the <u>star</u> <u>company</u> to take the place of Co A whose term expired the 5th of this month. You know Lewiston was always famous for great giving names as my Co when it first came out they named it "The Lewiston [*illegible*] Rifle Men" I enlisted one year ago last August for three years so you see I have already served 14 months of it. I will now close this very poor letter   Please excuse this poor envelope as it is all the kind I have   next time I write I think we shall be where I can get better stationary   I shall be anxious to hear from you and find out how you enjoy living in Lewiston once more. Dont fail to write soon

I remain as ever your True Friend
Abial H Edwards
H A Guard
1st Brig 1st Div 19th Corps
Via Washington D.C.

1. Brig. Gen. Alfred A. Torbert, commander of Sheridan's cavalry.

Cedar Creek Near Middleton. Va
October 15th 1864

My Dear Friend Anna

I will begin a letter to day to send you as the Mail leaves here very suddenly when it does go out. We have been having a little excitement here within a day or two. Thursday 13th The Rebels advanced to a hill this side of Strausburg 1 1/2 a mile [1.5 miles] from here and had quite a Battle. I had a splendid view of the Rebel Infantry their Batteries the men to work on their Cannon   I had a feild glass and could see them very plainly   the[re] was heavy cannonadeing all day but night closed and all fighting ceased. Yesterday morning we expected a big fight but the Rebels were very quiet nothing but a little skirmishing all day. Yesterday our folks captured a Guerrilla who deserted from a New York Reg- while we was at Harrissonburg and joined the Rebel Guerrillas   when our folks got him he acknowledged that he had already shot some of our men. he had on a suit of Rebel Grey and under that a union blue suit. Yesterday at 10 he was taken out close by our Head Quarters   a grave was dug a prayer offered by a Chaplain   the man stood at the head of his grave   eight Cavalry men then advanced and fired at him with their carbines and he fell back into his grave dead. He showed no sorrow for his crimes. This morning our Division went out and found the Rebels still in force near here. It will be hard to tell what will be done now. It is said that the Rebels have been heavily re enforced and it looks reasonable for they would not show such a bold front with only the army that we scattered. It has been very cold until to day   the sun shines brightly and it is very pleasant. Last evening was splendid   the bright moon made it nearly as light as day. You may be sure I thought of dear old Maine many a time during the evening   I suppose that you are enjoying your self nicely in Lewiston. You say you shall stop at the mill unless something turns up. I did not understand your meaning until the other day I got a letter from a friend of ours which gave me a slight idea. Now Anna I am a going to wish you heaps of happinness before hand   a great many of the Lewiston boys belonging to our Reg- who have been at home on furlough are now returning. I shall try and get a furlough this winter. Well I will now close until we get a mail in hopes to hear from you.

Ever Your True Friend Abial

Near Middleton, Va
October 16th 1864

My Dear Friend

Tis Sabbath beautiful sabbath when all worldly thoughts are supposed to be laid aside and rest for all. But how different it is here to day. Last night at 12 orders came to be in line to repel an attack from the Rebels at 5 this morning   Well morning came and the Rebels showed no disposition to fight us to day and so all day long our army has been to work digging rifle pits throwing up breast works etc   all the Generals are on the hills looking out for the work showing how important it is. It certainly looks as though they expected the Rebels to attack us here. With out doubt the Rebel army has been heavily re enforced and they may try to retrieve their fallen name   they are bold and saucy and I think we shall have hot work with them but we have great confidence in Sheriden and the army is in good spirrets over our victories and all seem willing to let the Rebels do their worst. How I should enjoy going to church in Lewiston to day. I miss the privilage of attending church more than any thing else   We ex-pect Mr Knox[1] out here daily   how glad we shall be to welcome him among us. Well I will write no more to night   I hope you are having a pleasant day Anna

From Abial

1. Rev. George Knox was killed in an accident a few weeks after this letter was written.

In camp near Midletown. Va.
H-d Qurs 1st Brig 1st Div
19th A. C.
October 21st 1864

My Dear Sister [Marcia]

Once more I am permited to write to you to let you know that I am alive. Oh Marcia that the scenes of the last few days could be shut out of my mind   another Battle[1] the most severe of any fought in the valley has been fought on the this very spot   at first it seemed as though it would be a defeat to us But our Brave Sheriden wrung a great victory from the very jaws of defeat. The 18th the Rebels was seen to be moving heavy colums over the mountain but Sheriden had gone to Washington leaving Wright[2] (6th Corps) Emory (19th) in command   On the 19th I was waked up about up about 5 in the morning by the war of musketry & artillary   I got up and soon it began to grow louder   the Rebels had got in the rear of the 8th Corps on our left and was advancing on us   by 6 in the morn the wounded began to go by our Quarters   we had received no orders to strike tents and soon the bullets began to spat all about us   we took our tents down and put them in the wagons   by this time the Rebels had captured our Breast works on the hill just above us   took a Bat-tery and turned it on us and as we started the teams they (the Rebels) formed a line on our right at our rear and sent the bullets all about us then the shells came in bursting all about us it was dredful. The[y] shot men all around us I started with one of our teams when they shot one of the mules on the team I stoped to see if we could start the team when a peice of shell came and hit one of the other mules on the team and we had to leave it as then the Rebels was comeing down on us on three sides I though[t] if we was not shot that we would be taken Prisoners sure one of the Div Guard just a head of us was killed one of our horses was killed. The 29th then came and advanced on the Rebels by this time the Rebels had captured all of our works 1st ME Battery and some other guns 5 of the 29th was shot before they left camp Capt Nye got his commission as Major the night before and comd the Reg Capt Kingsley of my Co got his commis and Serg⊥ C H Jumper[3] as 2nd Lieut Gen Sheriden was on his way back from Washington and hearing of the fight rode very hard until he got here about 10 A.M. He rode right on the feild told the boys they wasnt half whipped Turned on the Rebels drove them from our works way beyond fishers Hill Capturing hard up to 70 peices of Artillary Recaptured all of ours and some besides 14 Battle flags ambulances Wagons all their amunition all the Cannon they had and as yet we dont know the number of prisoners. Our Brigade was in the fight all day and lost heavy over 500 29th went in a little over 300 strong had 11 killed on the feild and 114 wounded besides a great many slightly wounded.[4] Major Nye wounded and Capt Kingsley wounded in My Co K 15 wounded Houghton Bond had his left arm taken of McLaughlin his right leg. Serg⊥ John A Willard wounded through the neck bad He has no use of his arms I went in the Hospital and fed him. The old 10th boys suffered dredfully many will die of their wounds. I have reason to thank God for my life. The tears would come when I stood over the poor boys who I have lived with for over 3 years. It looked <u>hard</u> <u>hard</u> Serg⊥ Osgood[5] is wounded If I was with the Co I should be the highest in rank for duty so you see how badly they was cut up My Co is so small I begin to think it my duty to go back to it Adj⊥ Gould wants me to stop here but I think I shall go to the Co soon. It makes me home sick to go to the Reg⊥ and see the vacant places Poor little Wetherall[6] of Naples they think was killed Our camp ground is strewn with graves. In our Teams that the Rebels got I lost my knapsack. A new pair of shoes 5.00 pair of gloves $2.00. $2.00 worth of paper & envelopes besides lot of other things. Adj Gould lost a box when we come back to our old ground I found my old bed of Cedor bushes full of Grape & Canister and pieces of shell. I will now close but will write soon again. Lot of 29th wounded will die. We have reason to be thankful for the Victory but oh will the people of the north realize can they realize the inhuman sight the suffering we saw. The Rebels robbed all of our wounded they could even striping them naked. I got your letter last night   Dont let [lose] that 100.00 I last sent you will you. Give my Love to all

Aff Brother
Abial

1. The Battle of Cedar Creek.
2. Maj. Gen. Horatio G. Wright.
3. Charles Henry Jumper.
4. Figures given in introduction for killed and wounded at Cedar Creek are accurate.
5. Pvt. Houghton Bond, Pvt. Tyler H. McLaughlin, 1st Sgt. John A. Willard, and Sgt. James A. Osgood recovered from their wounds.
6. William Wetherby of Naples [Maine] was killed at Cedar Creek. There is no Wetherall on the rolls of the regiment.

In Camp Near Middletown. VA.
Co K 29th ME Reg⊥
Oc⊥ 22nd 1864

My Dear Anna

Your kind letter of the 17th was received to night and read with much pleasure and I will now attempt to answer it. I am very sorry to think you have the idea that I am tired of corrisponding with you far from it. I look as eagerly for your letters as I do my sisters and if there is any one tired of writeing I am afraid it is you.

Since I wrote to you last we have had a very severe Battle and as usual been victorious. Early on the morning of the 18th the Rebels surprised us and until 10 A.M. had all about their own way. before we took our tents down they fired at us and the shells screeched around us pretty lively   They took most of the 1st ME Battery   But after this they were done our folks takeing 51 peices of Cannon from them the most of their Amanition Ambulances 14 Battle flags & hosts of prisoners. The 29th was in the fight all day and lost heavy   They went in between 3 & 400 strong and had 10 killed 114 wounded many severely besides th[ere] was but few escaped slight wounds & marks. In the morning the Rebels occupied the feild and robbed our dead & wounded of all their valuables. My Company had 15 wounded most of them severe   Major G H Nye was wounded also Capt A E

106

Kingsley of K   The Rebels got totaly routed and drove beyond Strausbury   Our Chaplain Mr. Knox is here   he got here the night before the Battle   one of our teems had 2 mules shot so we could not get it of the feild   all my things was in it so I lost all my clothing Port folio e c. But I dont mind this much as long as the Johnies got the worst of it. We are now encamped on our same old ground but th[ere] is many vacant places and our camps are strewn with little mounds which contain both friend and foe. Please excuse very short letter Anna as the mail is going right away and as it only goes out every 2 days I am anxious to send this now. Dont fail to write as soon as you get this. For I am anxious to hear from you.

Ever your True Friend
Abial

Addressed to: Mrs. Jordan Cook[1]
Casco Maine
Nov 8th 1864

This morning we got orders to be ready to march at day light struck tents but did not move. Our folks expected an attack by the Rebels as General Emory's scouts came in last night and reported them advancing this way heavily reenforced. We are ready for them at any time as our Generals are determined not to be surprised again. Well we voted to day for President & Governor. I voted for Portland and had the privilage of voting for Pres Lincoln & Gen Conly.[2] Our reg⊥ stood 174 for Lincoln & 40 for McLelean   I am sorry to see so many votes for him. I dont think I shall ever forget my first voting   we voted after the tents was down expecting an attack as much as could be. I threw my votes with as good a will as I ever did any thing in my life. The men that voted for MC in my opinnion voteing for one thing and fighting for another. I think some of them are ashamed of it even now. Tis eve now raining hard and as muddy as it can be real Virginnia blacking. We are looking anxiously for Gen Beal to get back. I have been thinking to night of Mr Knox thinking of the few sermons he preached to us after he joined us and when I think how thouroughly patriotic he was how much at heart he had the good of his country I think he felt willing to give up his life for his country   in his last sermon to us he paid a nobel compliment to Pres Lincoln. It did our boys good to have such a man to preach to them. He took the hearts of the men by storm and as short as time as he had been with us he was loved by all. Every day shows us what a great loss we have met with But we can truly say "Our loss is his gain" Well no more to night

From Brother

Abial

1. Mrs. Jordan Cook was Abial's sister Marcia.
2. Samuel Cony was the successful candidate of the Republicans for Governor of Maine. He won two successive elections. "I voted for Portland" means that Abial carried the totals of those voting absentee from Portland to the headquarters.

Near Newtown, VA.

Nov 14th 1864

My Dear Anna

Your very kind letter of the 6th was received to day was much pleased to hear from you. This week has been very exciting for us as the Rebels have been very near two days fighting in sight of our entrenchments. Yesterday our Brigade went out & drove them 3 miles 29th had one wounded Barton Ross of Lewiston. The Rebel Army has been reenforced & now numbers 30,000. Ewell[1] has relieved Early and Sheriden has received information that they will attack us at an early day. If they do it will be a hard fight Major Nye is so that recommands the Reg$^{\perp}$ Anna I voted in the feild and had th[e] great privilage of voting for Lincoln. No Anna I do not desire the war to last 4 years longer. Neither do I want a peace that would disgrace us as a nation. What does MC- surporters say. That us soldiers have not gained any thing or done any thing in the feild. Can we vote for such men. No Anna I want an honorable peace and until we do get it I am willing to serve my country in the feild. Let Volandigham and such men do all they can They only serve to make the soldier Truer to his country than ever before. I detest them and their principals. I can show a private in the C.G. service <u>some respect</u> but such men as they are <u>none</u> Well Anna you say your birth day has passed now I want to make you a birthday present if it is late but as we are situated so that I cant buy any thing I will send you 10 dollars buy what you like with it and consider it a birth day present from Abial Also you will find enclosed a two dollar bill. please buy me a book and send it by mail. as we want reading matter sadly. I want no particular book so will let you make your own choice. Please write as soon as you get this. Please excuse here as the mail goes out

this eve next time I will do better   29th Maine voted 174 for Lincoln
40 for McL. <u>Didnt we do well</u>   Well Anna <u>we wont disaggree any</u>
<u>more on politics will we</u>

Good Night
Ever Thy Friend
Abial

1. Confederate Lt. Gen. Richard S. Ewell.

Camp Russell. Shenandoah Valley
Dec 1st 1864

My Dear Anna.

Your welcome letter of Nov 25th is before me and I now hasten to
answer it. I was much pleased to hear from you   As for that Birth
day present if you had not accepted it I should certainly been of-
fended. The Book I sent for I had no choice in for I should have left
it for you to select but as you have returned the money I have not a
word to say. I would much rather that you had used the money to have
got the book. Many thanks for that waverly. I like that paper very
much. I am still at Brigade Head Quarters. For the last week we have
been very buisy in building log huts   we build them about four feet
high and have a cozy little fire place   for boards we tear down dwell-
ing houses whose owners have deserted them and gone to Richmond
& now we have very comfortable winter Quarters. But at present
many are doubtful as to our occupying them long. We are very anxious to hear some thing reliable from Gen Sherman   when I look at
his move and see how he has cut him self from all communications
with the world and trusted him self as he has it looks to me like the
grandest move ever made. God grant that he may be Victorious.[1] If
we have got to have a winter campaign I am ready for it. Union troops
with their trusty muskets will earn a quicker more lasting Peace than
the Chicago Convention & Jeff Davises Cabinet ever could aggree upon   How I should like to be in old Maine New Years. Which I think
will be extremely doubtful as all furloughs are stoped for the present.
I will not write a long letter to night as the mail leaves early in the
morning but will endeavor to do better next time. Dont fail to write
often.

From Your True Friend
Abial H Edwards.
K 29th Maine.

1. Maj. Gen. William T. Sherman had cut his communications on his "march
to the sea" from Atlanta to Savannah. He was soon to emerge and capture Savannah
before Christmas.

                                        Camp Russell
                                        Dec 11th 1864
Anna
    Enclosed find pen & case   Please accept it as a Christmas Gift
from
                                        Abial
PS   This may be received before Christmas   if so you can use it for
my benefit on that day
                                        Abial

                                        Camp Russell. Va
                                        Dec 17th 1864
Friend Anna
    Your beautiful gift "[*illegible*] came to night   How can I suffi-
ciently thank you for it. I know I shall like it for I have heard it spo-
ken highly of but never saw if before. Many Many Thanks. To day has
been very lively here   a salute of 100 guns was fired in honor of Gen
Thomas Victory over Hood.[1] Truly the Rebels are badly used every
where. God bless the Noble Generals that are doing so much as well
as their armies. Never has the Union armies had more encouragement
to persever then now. I feel more Patriotic than ever. I want to come
to Maine this winter very much but as yet do not know if I shall be
able to. The[re] is no snow here now and it is very pleasant   As for
news all we get here is war news. I shall not be able to write much
of a letter as I wrote to you day before yesterday so will close by wishing you a Mery Christmas. Write soon.
                                    From Your Friend
                                    Abial. H. Edwards.

    1. Maj. Gen. George H. Thomas defeated John B. Hood's Confederates at
Franklin, south of Nashville, on November 30, and again on December 15 just
outside of Nashville. Hood's army was destroyed.

                                        Camp Russell, Va.
                                        H-d. Div. 1st Brigade 1st Div
                                        19th A. C.
                                        Dec 21st/64
My Dear Friend
    Takeing a little leisure time that is now offered me I thought I
could improve it in no better way than in writeing to you. Tis a bitter

cold night   The wind is whistling round our little houses in the vain endeavor to force an entrance   the[re] is now about 3 inches of snow but the next warm day will cause it to disappear   The[re] has been some changes here since I wrote to you last   the 8th Corps has all left here   report has it that they have gone to reenforce Grant   if so the 19th Corps is all that the[re] now is in Shenandoah Valley. Yesterday the 2nd Brigade of our Division went back to Summits Point 9 miles nearer Harpers Ferry and it is thought that we shall go back in a day or so. General Beal has been promoted full Brigadier and Major Nye is to be Colonel of our Reg. and our Adj. J. M. Gould is to be Major all of which pleases the members of the Reg- much. Our new Chaplain has come and had services last Sabbath for the first time   We like him very well but still we all feel that he cant fill Mr. Knoxes place. His name is Webster[1] of Lewiston a Universalist I beleive   Do we not have glorious news from our armies of the west   now they all seem to have taken up Sheriden's plan and fought the rebels with a "vim" as Sheriden says   If they still keep on whipping them I shall begin to think that this war is really a going to end sometime   I understand that the President has called for 300,000 more men   I am glad of it   let him have enough next spring and then begin and carry this war to a speedy & glorious end. I have began to think that I can not have a furlough this winter as all the armies seem to be moving and we are subject to the same orders that all the rest are that is to be ready to move any time   therefore they will want all the well Soldiers in the feild. How I should like to be in the Pine Tree State Christmas but I find it is no use wishing for what is an impossibility   How cold it must be for our "boys" in the Hospitals in Augusta. I am not sorry that we are not there now. Well Anna I will close my poor letter. Would that I could write you more interesting ones. Please excuse all mistakes and write soon to your

> True Friend
> Abial
> Dec 25th 1864[2]

Dear Friend

   Tis a splendid day for Christmas warm and pleasant. I can imagine what a pleasant time you are having to day. I got that Literary companion[3] you sent me   Many Many Thanks. Please write to me soon and let me know how you have enjoyed Christmas.

> Abial

1. Charles J. Webster.

2. Abial added this letter to the previous one dated Dec. 21, 1864.
3. *The Literary Companion* was a popular anthology-type magazine.

Casco [Maine] Jan 8th 1865
Dear Anna
I have got a furlough for 20 days   I got up here to my Sisters
Friday but have not been out of the house since I got here   I have
had the erisisifilas [erysipelas] in my neck of the worst kind. But I
think I shall be over to Lewiston Saturday next   I shall call at No 5
Hill Block as I suppose that you are there still. I thought I would
write a note to let you know I was here as I got my furlough very
unexpectedly

With Love
Your Friend
Abial

Portland. Home. Wends Eve
Jan 18th 1865
Dear Anna
I will write you a note to night to send with "Enoch Aeden". I
hope the book will suit you I like it very much   "The Grand-
Mother"¹ I think very pretty   Oh <u>what</u> a <u>time</u> I had to get over to
Casco Sunday   if I had waited 'till afternoon I could not have got
home that day as it was I was almost froze and had to walk part of the
way. I start for the army Friday morn   only one day and as much as
<u>40</u> relatives I have got to visit in that one day   If I had only had 40
days it would have suited me better   Please write very soon and direct the same as ever.
   Please excuse short note and when I <u>get</u> <u>home</u> to Va I will try and
write a longer one

With Love
I Remain
Abial H. Edwards.
K 29th Me.

1. *Enoch Arden* was a very popular collection of poems by Alfred Tennyson published in 1864. "The Grandmother" was one of them.

Camp Sherriden [Virginia]
Jan 31st 1865

Dear Sister [Marcia]

i will write you a short note to night to let you know how prospering.

Gould[1] has gone home and I have had charge of the Guard 48 men and with drawing their rations it has kept me pretty buisy But last night Gen Beal called me in and apointed me Brigade Mail Agent. Aint that good I had rather have it than be Serg. In fact all other Brigades have Serg's for that business. I have a horse to ride and everything in good shape. It is one of the best positions in the Brigade for an enlisted man nothing to do but to see to the mail. So to morrow morning I shall turn over to another Corporal and commence on my new duty. Gen Beal told his AAAG that I took care of his mail in the 10th Maine and now he wanted me to take care of his Brigade Mail. Everynight our mail numbers from 500 to 1000 letters and 2 or 300 papers for 6 Reg's numbering about 4000 men so you see it is quite a post office

Well I will close

Goodnight
Abel

1. Maj. John M. Gould, the regimental adjutant (and historian).

Camp Sherriden. Va.
Febuary 2nd 1865

Dear Anna

Having a few leisure moments to night I thought I could improve them in no better way then in writeing to you It has been very pleasant to day a real spring day. I had a ride on horse back which I enjoyed very much. Since I got back I have been very buisy. The Serg' of our Guard has gone home on furlough and I have had charge of the Guard 42 men that with drawing their rations has kept me very buisy. yesterday General Beal told me that he had appointed me Mail Agent for the Brigade and so to morrow I shall take that place. I know I shall like the work very much. I shall have a horse of my own and what is better be my own Master. I have six Reg's & 3 Batteries whose Mail comes here. I have to sort this and they come to me after it Every night I have about 2 bushels of papers & letters to take care of all the way from 500 to 1000 letters every night besides the papers so that you see I have quite a Post Office. Yesterday the[re] was a Cavalry Review. Oh it was grand three Divisions of Cavalry was [*burned*] but the greatest attraction was the crowd of stars with their staffs. The Generals were all togather. The[re] was Major General Sherriden, Emory, Custer[1] & Torbert[2] Brigadier Generals Beal, McMillin,[3] Fessenden,[4] Davis[5] & several others The[re] is no prettier sight in the army than a body of Cavalry. And our Cavalry here have earned a name that is imperrishable for bravery. There was a rumor of our going to Savannah but within a few days nothing has been said so I think that is done with for the present. I hope so. Anna I suppose you are enjoying the privelage of going to School How I wish I was there to attend wouldnt we be diligent Scholars. But I fear that my School days have gone for ever gone. Mr. Webster has been very still lately holding no meetings of any kind. I under stand that he does not favor evening meetings. that is Prayer meetings I think he is wrong For if an evening meeting does no good it surely does no harm. And in such a place as this where the soldier has so much spare time by attending such meetings it may keep them from mischief. He's not the man to suit me although he is a very eloquent preacher we need something besides that in the army We need a man that has got a heart in his work. Well I will now close my dry very dry letter. Write often Anna

From
Abial

1. Maj. Gen. George A. Custer, commander of the Third Division.
2. Brig. Gen. Alfred T. A. Torbert, commander of Sheridan's cavalry.
3. Brig. Gen. James W. McMillin, commander of the First Division.
4. Brig. Gen. James Deering Fessenden.
5. Brig. Gen. Edwin P. Davis, commander of the First Brigade of the First Division.

Camp Sherriden, Va
Febuary 5th 1865

My Dear Anna

I will write a few words this afternoon to let you know how we are getting along in "Dixie." T's a cold windy day and very lonely. This morning we had Brigade Review & Inspection—but it was so cold that the[re] was little pleasure in it. Since I came back I have charge of the Brigade Mail for six Reg's & 9 Batteries among the Batteries is the 1st Maine. I like my duties very much I have a nice tent all to my self & a horse to ride. By the way you probably have seen <u>Great</u>

<u>Rumors</u> of <u>Peace</u>. We hear some thing about it every day but I think that Gen Sherman & Terry[1] with other Generals are moveing the surest Peace Commissioners twords Richmond   I think their colums of tried veterans will do more twords Peace then a whole army of Blairs[2] & [*illegible*] in their style of Peace Makeing. Our 2nd Div is now in Savannah and that City is now commanded by General Cavier Grover of Maine   I hardly think that we shall go there at present. I hope not for I am very well satisfied here. Time passes away very pleasantly in reading writing and with what light duties I have to do. I was at the Depot yesterday as the train came in and saw Gen Sherriden's Spy   She is a young Lady about 20 years of age. She ranks as Major wearing a Majors shoulder straps and jacket   she is very beautiful with a very independent manner as though she was capable of depending upon herself   She has already been noted for her great brasen in going into the Rebel lines through their armies and as yet she has never been caught. A female Rebel Spy was caught here last Friday   I dont know what they intend to do with her   she was dressed in a soldiers suit of blue. We some expect our Band to go home on a short furlough   if they do they will take their instruments with them   some of the people will have a rich treat to hear them   It is a splendid Band and is called the best in the Corps. Please write soon Anna   Excuse all imperfections

From Thy Friend
Abial H. Edwards
Direct to Head Quarters 1st Brigade
1st Division 19th A C
via Washington D. C.

1. Maj. Gen. Alfred Terry who led a successful assault on Fort Fisher in January, 1865. This led to the loss by the Confederates of Wilmington, North Carolina, which had been the last major port not closed by the Union naval blockade.

2. Francis P. Blair, prominent old Jacksonian and patriarch of a powerful political family, was allowed by Lincoln to travel to Richmond to see what kind of a peace Jefferson Davis would accept. This led to the unsuccessful Hampton Roads conference on February 3, 1865.

Camp Sherriden Va.
Febuary 18th 1865

My Dear Anna
Your kind favor of the 13th was received last night [*line burned*] to hear from you. It had been so long since I had received a letter from you I was afraid you had been sick. It is very lonesome here now &

very quiet. The Rebels are very quiet even the Guerrilles have forgot to molest us for the last week. But it is the quiet just before the storm. I imagine a few months from now will open one of the greatest campaigns this army ever saw. Each side is prepareing for the contest. and all is wanted now is setteled weather and good travelling which we hardly ever have until the first of May. I like my new duties very much My Mail. I take care of is for the Brigade Head Quarters. The Pioneer Corps of 1st Brig. 153rd New York, 116th New York, 114th New York, 90th New York [*line burned*] Brigade Head Quarters 1st Maine Battery, 5th New York Battery. 1st Rhode Island Battery. You see that I have a <u>right</u> <u>smart</u> <u>lot</u> of Mail to distribute. One night we judged the[re] was 3,000 letters besides newspapers packages & I have a mail come in once a day and one goes out. You would smile to see the packages that come for the soldiers by Mail. Here is a sample Boots, Tobacco, Coffee, Tea, pepper, pills, powders jack knifes, thread socks slippers pants coats vests hats caps etc. etc. You can judge what a lot of such articles is sent. One night I was distributing the mail   General Beal was in my tent and as I empted a bag of mail on the floor the[re] was one letter filled with cayenne pepper which broke [*line burned*] it flew all around and was so very strong that it filled the tent. It got us all crying & sneezing. The General really used <u>profane</u> <u>language</u>. It made him sneeze so that I had to laugh at him   we had to leave the tent until it got setteled. It is really amuseing to me to see the different packages sent by mail.

I enjoy riding horse back very much   I have a fine horse and when I have the blues I ride out two or three miles and come back feeling much better. They still continue giving out furloughs to our Regs. Only think I have one year & six months longer to serve   how time flies   I have been in Uncle Sams Service now 3 years & six months. That is in the 10th Maine & 29th. I am really ashamed to send you such a poor letter Anna

write but you must accept the will for the deed. I will now close

> Please write soon & often
> From Your True Friend
> Abial H. Edwards
> 1st Brig 1st Div 19th A C

Camp Sherridan. VA.
Febuary 26th 1865

My Dear Anna.

Takeing the opportunity now offered me I will write you a few lines hopeing they may prove acceptable. Tis a lovely day much like spring   we have here & there a spot of snow but the most of it has disappeared and the little birds are carrying the songs all around us. While all other [*illegible*] are buisy dealing out just retribution to the dastard Rebels we are lying here idle. But I fancy it will be but a little while longer. They seem to be fitting up for a move from here shortly. Last week they sent up a new Potomic train and Madam Rumor has it that Hancocks[1] new corps is to join us in the valley. If so we shall have quite an army to start Richmond way with as th[ere] is about 40,000 Cavalry now here. Since we have had an indication of early spring the Rebel Guerrilla's have began to trouble us again   Last week they captured 2 of our Major Generals from us (Crook[2] & Kelley[3]) and yesterday they captured a few men from our Brigade that was out chopping wood. One fellow was cutting wood and a Rebel rode up to him & made him give him his money & watch & then left him. But he was satisfied to get of as easily as that. Yesterday I had a sketch of our Quarters here taken and shall send it to Portland to be Photographed by my friend Mr. Lewis   if it proves a good picture I will send you one which I think it will. By the way I saw some verses yesterday called "Enoch Arden boiled down"   That is the whole Poem condensed in six verses   I wish I had them to send you   It took a very matter of fact view of Enoch's trials. This week past I have been kept pretty buisy. fortunately Sundays I have nothing to do as no mail goes out or comes. What mail I have to take care of I find is all I want to do. Our Division Post Master is a man from Lewiston   his name is Arthur T Jacobs he used to own a dry goods store on Lisbon Street. They have now stoped all furloughs from this army which proves they are getting ready to move   Havent we been having glorious news for the last few weeks   Charleston the hot bed of treason in our posession.[4] The Old Flag once more waving over Sumter Wilmington in our possession with a promise that Mobil will soon be and all this with but little blood shed. Truly we ought to be thankful   The Rebels are fast comeing to grief and I see their <u>dear</u> <u>friends</u> of the North hase but little to say now a days. I really think they are beginning to see the error of their ways and are repenting. I hope so. They are fast filling up the 29th Maine with Recruits   Some are comeing every week. Let them come and be in the ranks to help deal the last blow to this unholy Rebellion. I think that this year will be the last of this war and we have every reason for beleiving so. I have yesterdays daily before me and it says the two last days that the[re] was 800 Rebel Deserters came in & gave them selves up takeing an oath of alleigence. If they continue to do so it will hurt Lee's Army more than a great battle would by far. Deserters are also comeing in to our lines here in the valley very fast and wretched looking objectors they are   shoeless without Over coats or blankets they are to be pitied. As soon as they take the oath of alleigance to the United States they are sent North and there they procure employment. As I sit here writeing I can hear the Pickets fireing   the Guerrillas are troubleing them and the[re] has been fireing for the last two hours but it will not amount to much   they probably are trying for a weak place in the Picket line so as to make a dash in and do what mischief they can. The Sergaent of our Guard was at home on 20 day furlough and got married   he married a Mis Susan A Wheelwright of Lewiston. He was very still about it but we found out in time. His name is Geo H Gould   I think I will now close for fear of tireing you   I shall call this a very dry letter and I think you will before you finish reading it. Please excuse errors and write soon and often

From Your True Friend
Abial H. Edwards
Head Quarters 1st Brig 1st Div
19th A

1. Maj. Gen. Winfield S. Hancock.
2. Brig. Gen. George Crook.
3. Brig. Gen. B. F. Kelley. He and Crook were soon released.
4. Charleston, cut off by Sherman's army in the rear, was evacuated by the Confederates on February 18, 1865.

Camp Sherridan. VA.
March 7th 1865

My Dear Friend
Your kind missive was received to night and as usual I was much pleased to hear from you. Since I wrote to you last we have been very buisy fitting up for our spring campaign which will probably commence very soon. Gen Sherridan has gone down the valley with all of our Cavalry and captured old Gen Jubal Early and all his force then with him   1,800 what was left went into Richmond with out any arms   Lee sent up 4 Brigades and they will probably come this way. We have been expecting an attack here every night but have not been troubled yet. Rebels have been seen neer our Picket line. Th[ere] is no snow here at all & the little Robins have been favoring us with a visit. It is very muddy here however and it will take some time for the ground to be setteled. One of my Brothers has enlisted and is in Portland in camp   My youngest Brother 16 years old tried to go but they would not accept him for which I feel very thankful.[1] He was very

much disappointed in not going. My oldest Brother is now 20 years old. he says he likes a soldiers life very much until he enlisted[2]   I was fortunate in not having any neer ~~friends~~ (I would say relatives) for I have many dear friends in the army. While I was at home I was looking over many of my Photographs (in all I have over 100) many th[ere] was among them whose face I shall see no more. several were killed before Petersburg   others was laid away in the low lands of Lousiana   other there were that rest in the Shenandoah valley free from all earthly troubles. It was a pleasure to look on the pictoral faces of the friends gone before but still it caused many a heart ache to think we shall meet them no more. America how many priceless jewels have been offered up to Thee   how many have given life that thy name might continue with the other great nations of earth   I am eager for our spring campaign to Commence. Not knowing what it has in store for me. yet I feel anxious to be at work to know that we are helping in the great struggle that is surely breaking up the Rebellion. God has dealt kindly with me he has preserved life & health through all the hardships of camp life and I can truly say I feel thankful. The ensueing summer has much in store for us. Yet I would not cast aside the veil that shrouds it from our view   time will bring it to us in its own time and we should be content. I will now close   Please excuse my <u>very poor letter</u> and I shall be happy to heer from you Soon

> Thy friend
> Abial

1. Philip Wadleigh Edwards.
2. Bela Edwards.

> Camp Sherridan, Va.
> March 20th 1865

My Dear Anna

I will take a few leisure moments this eve to write to you hopeing it may prove acceptable. I should have wrote before but Friday I & a friend of mine got to raceing horses and in jumping a ditch mine stumbled & fell throwing me quite a distance but fortunately not hurting me very bad only makeing me very sore & lame for a day or two   I have concluded not to jump ditches any more until I get a horse that can do it readily. We are having such splendid weather now beautiful spring is really here and as friend said to day we are having real '<u>home sick weather</u>'. I thought no no other words could express it better for when it is so very pleasant it makes one think of home often, very often. My Brother[1] has come out here in the 15th Maine   he got here yesterday and we had a pleasant time I assure you although I am very sorry he is in the army   I shall try and make the best of it thinking it all for the best. The[re] is a rumor here to night that the Rebels have sent a force up this way   a few days will prove wether it is false or no   The 29th had a lot of Recruits to night   we shall shortly have a full Reg-

The[re] is not much transpireing here at present & I must confess that the time drags heavily very often. It seems to me that you are one of my corrospondents that begin to drop of by degrees   I hope not certainly Anna. I had a letter from a little Coz in Portland Saturday night and I find she is to be married soon   then poor me will get no more letters from her. Now if I should be served so by you Anna I should feel badly. I find letters from friends are more precious than any thing else can be for us in the army. I saw General Hancock & Family to night   he has a fine looking family I assure you. They have come up here to see him   also General Emorys Family are here. I will now close hopeing to hear from thee oftener than I have of late I remain

Thy True Friend,
Abial

1. Bela.

Camp Sherridan, Va.
April 2nd 1865

My Dear Friend Anna

Your kind letter reached me last night & I now hasten to answer it. Many thanks for that pretty little pin cushion. It is very useful I assure you. Oh what a lovely day. as warm as mid summer   The[re] has been a salute fired here to day in honor of [*burned*] in the Potomac Army & Sherridan. The[re was] very hard fighting and still they are fighting   May God help the right. If victory is ours I think the Rebels will see the folly of fighting longer. They are completely discouraged now and well they might be. Then you say you are going back to Lewiston this summer. I hope you will enjoy your self there. Our Chaplain is now at home on a furlough. It wouldnt make much difference to the Reg' if he remained at home. He is not the man we want   A Reg' needs a Chaplain that they can love not one who cares nothing for them. I think we shall leave here in a very few days now as they are getting already for a move. It is thought that we shall go down the valley twords Richmond the boys are all anxious to commence a campaign I just got a letter from my sister & she says that out of the 10 who enlisted in my old school district last spring. One short year ago The[re] is just [*burned*] he returned home last week a Paroled Prisoner. Having been with the rest & taken care of them until they were at rest. Starvation wounds & Prison fare finished their sufferings Anna sometimes I can't imagine why it is that I am spared when so many of my friends not serving one third of the time I have are gone. never to return How my heart aches when I think of them. For few a very few can prize friends more highly then I and when I think of them as gone for ever gone it seems cruel. But I know they have a crown of glory in the bright world above & where no more the roar of battle & the dreadful carnage of the Battle feild can trouble them. I shall have to make this letter short as I have got to go away this afternoon I will write again soon I think [*burned*] week I shall get those pictures of our camp ground then I will send you one [*burned*]

Thy Aff Brother
Abial

April 3rd 1865

Darling Anna

Enclosed is a very small picture of our Head Quarters. I will send you a larger one soon Great excitement to night 35,000 Rebels reported within 9 miles of us comeing this way

Excuse haste
Aff Abial

Camp Near Winchester, VA.
April 9th 1865

My Dear Anna

I will write you a few lines to day hopeing they may prove acceptable. We are now encamped on the out skirts of Winchester on the very ground where the 10th Maine first met the Rebels. One year ago to day we was in the Battle of Pleasant Hill. how changed since then. now we can look to a glorious end of the Rebellion. Our Head Quarters is in the yard of a fine old Virginnia Mansion. The Peach trees are in full bloom and it looks very pleasant I assure you We are now already to move where ever they want us and are waiting orders. I hardly think we shall stop in the valley but go some where where we are needed. probably join the Potomac Army. How glorious that noble army must feel the privilage of going in to the Rebel Capitol of doing what they have done.¹ They say the people of the North are very happy over the news   if so how happy the army is who have <u>more</u> cause to rejoice. I will confess Anna I saw more than one soldier shed tears of joy when the glorious news of Victory reached us. I feel now my last 4 years of labor & hardships have not been in vain. I can look back on them & say truly I am satisfied although th[e] best years of my life. They are given freely to the great cause   Thank God my Love of Country has never failed me in defeet or victory   Sometimes I have thought my life has been to firmly wedded to the army   be it as it may I can not regret it. It certainly will be the happiest moment of my life to have peace declared and this summer I surely think will see the happy event. Please excuse short letter this time as I have got to go out on Review this afternoon   I will write soon again. Please write soon again. We have been very buisy this last week moving twice and I have had all I could do to keep the mail along with us

> From Thy Friend
> Abial
> 1st Brigade Dwights Division²
> Army of Shenandoah

1. On April 2–3, 1865, Lee and the Confederate army evacuated Richmond. On the day that Edwards wrote this letter, Lee surrendered to Grant at Appomatox Court House.

2. The division commanded by Brig. Gen. William Dwight.

PART SIX

Lincoln's Death and the Grand Review

INTRODUCTION

The war ended with Edwards and the Twenty-ninth Maine still in the Shenandoah Valley. Here they received the sad news of the assassination of President Abraham Lincoln, which had a profound effect on Edwards. The Nineteenth Corps, of which they were a part, then moved to camps near Washington. While en route they saw Lincoln's funeral train and on arrival the Capitol covered with crepe.

On May 23 and 24, before most of the volunteers were mustered out, there was a Grand Review in Washington with 200,000 soldiers passing before the largest crowd the city had ever seen. On the first day the eastern armies, the Army of the Potomac and the Army of the Shenandoah, neat and precise, Edwards riding with General Beal at the head of his brigade, passed the reviewing stand before President Andrew Johnson, General Grant, the cabinet, and other notables. It was, Edwards told his sister, "the greatest day of my life." The next day Sherman's western armies, rough and tattered, strode past the same notables.

Reflecting on his wartime experiences Edwards concluded: "The Army has been a grand school to foster one[']s best impulses[.] here he has learned the best & most useful lessons of life & we can go back to a citizen[']s life feeling proud of our position in the years of 61–5." But it would be another year before he would return home. The Nineteenth Corps was ordered south on occupation duty.

BIBLIOGRAPHIC NOTE

There are vivid accounts of the Grand Review in Allan Nevins, *The War for the Union*, volume 4 (New York: Charles Scribner's Sons, 1971), pp. 364–67; and Shelby Foote, *The Civil War: A Narrative*, volume 3 (New York: Random House, 1974), pp. 1014–17.

Summits Point, Va
April 16th 1865

Dear Anna

Thy kind letter reached me this day   many thanks for your kind wishes. We had started for Lynchburg when the news came that Richmond had fallen & Lee surrendered when we returned to this place. Yesterday we received the sad news of Presidents Lincolns Assassination causing intense excitement and such gloom as I have rarely seen in the Army. How hard when he has just began to see the fruits of his labor to be taken away. I cant realize that we have lost our noble President. It has turned our rejoicing into mourning   Truly "His ways are mysterious & past finding out"   God grant that the Demon may be caught & be killed by slow torture   never have I seen such heart felt sorrow prevade every countenance as does now. Nothing else is talked about. In this great sorrow our victrys are rarely spoke of. Such bursts of indignation was never heard & should this army ever be called to meet the foe the spirrit of revenge would help them on   such kindness has the President has shown the Rebels I hope will never be shown them again. Let them suffer for their feindish deeds. I think we shall remain here for some time   now all are looking anxiously to see what Johnson will do. The Rebels probably think that they helped them selves when Lincoln was assassinated but they have hurt them selves. for Vice Pres Johnson has a will that will soon show them they have not helped their unholy cause. Revenge is the cry in the army & by all. Dear Anna you may think this a wild letter but really I have felt so bad to day I could not collect my thoughts sufficient to write clearest. Let me think of any thing else & my mind instantly returns to our dredful loss. Please excuse me Anna and I will try & do better next time. Please write soon and often   Hopeing to have the privilege of seeing you by the 4th of next July. With the privilege of knowing that our noble banner is floating over every portion of the United States is my earnest prayer

With Love I Remain
Abial

Tennallytown, D.C.
Quarters 1st Brig 1st Div 19th
April 22nd 1865

My Dear Sister [Marcia]
We received orders very suddenly at 12 midnight Thursday to be
ready to move   We took the cars¹ and got into Washington 10 A.M.
yesterday. about 8 miles out of Washington we met the funeral train
of the President   it was the gloomiest sight I ever saw   the train was
decorated with flags covered with crape and the car in which his body
was was completely covered just like a hearse   It looked sad. after we
got in we marched by the white house that was completely covered
with crape also War Department. The Capitol was also covered with
crape   I went all through the Capitol every room was craped from
Senate Chamber down. Every private house is trimmed in crape.
Such was the demand for crape that they used the market up & had
to buy black cambric. We had our flags trimed with crape   Indeed it
is the saddest sight I ever saw & I pray God I may never see the sight
again   We saw General Grant yesterday   he is quite young looking.
I have to go into Washington after our mail every day   We have got
a splendid camp ground I dont know how long we shall remain here.
The old Potomic Army is on the move now   Every flag is at half
mast. Every thing & every body is mourning mourning   Bela is here
& getting along nicely. I will write more soon   Aff Thine in haste
Brother
Abial

1. Train cars.

Tenallytown, Md.
Quarters of 1st Brig 1st Div
19th HQ
April 24th 1865

My Dear Anna
Your kind and thrice welcome letter reached me to night and I was
much pleased to hear from you. We have left the Shenandoah Valley.
Last Thursday we received orders to leave and started for Washington   we came all the way by cars. We reached Washington Friday
morning at 10. At 9 A.M. we met the train having the body of President Lincoln   its was covered with flags heavily draped with crape,
also the cars   the car in which his body was placed was draped like
a hearse. I never saw a more gloomy sight in my life & I pray God I
may never see such a sight again. All public houses & private are

draped in mourning   all flags are at half mast. trimmed with crape.
I was all through the capitol building   every room from senate
chamber down was creped   We passed the white house & War De-
partments both presented a gloomy sight I assure you. On our way
out here to camp we met General Grant with only one orderly with
him   he is a much younger man than I expected to see   He has now
gone down to join Sherman   We are out 5 miles from Washington
and I have to go in every day after our mail either on horse or in ambulance. It is a very pleasant ride. I do not know how long we shall
remain here   I hope we shall for the present. Every body seems to
like the course of President Johnson so far very well. You spoke of his
bearing the name of "Drunkerd Johnson"   If I have been informed
rightly he has never appeared in public but once the worse for rum
and that was the last 4th of March   he has since then signed a pledge
and has done nobly.¹ I hope that he will carry out Pres Lincoln's best
policy in every way. & let all traitors learn that they have got to bow
before the government they have abused & woe to the copper heads
that show their delight at the Pres death before any soldiers as a few
of the low minded have done. Please excuse poor letter Anna for I
have very poor accommodations this time   I will endeavor to do better next time   I have got to go to the city right away so shall have to
close

> Please write soon & often

Aff
Abial

1. Lincoln's successor, Andrew Johnson, when inaugurated as vice president in
the Senate chamber in March 1865, took a drink to steady himself before the cer-
emony, and it hit him very hard, causing gossip that he was a drunkard. Actually,
Johnson drank infrequently and in moderation. See photo 17 showing letter.

Near Washington D,C,
May 4th 1865

My Dear Anna

Your kind and thrice welcome of the 29th arrived last night and I
now hasten to answer it. We are now very pleasantly camped about 3
miles from the city and I have to go in daily after our mail and find
it a very pleasant ride. You say the soldiers must be very happy   they
are   words cannot convey the feelings of those who have risked life on
so many bloody feilds of battle. Yes the war is ended   "Peace on
earth good will to man"   No more blood shed No more struggles
with traitors. For they are conquered in every sense of the word   Not

however until they have robbed us of our Noble Leader. It seems as though we have been to happy over our recent victories and when that blow came it was indeed hard. Every building from the capitol with its long pennons of crepe to th[e] low hovel of the negro with its small piece of black cloth testify to the grief felt in this city for our beloved President   You thought I should be at home by the 4th of July. I hardly think so   No troops will be discharged until after all of our victorious armies comes to Washington and meet together. Then there is to be a Grand Review of the whole great Union Army that is to be mustered out   Probably it will be the greatest thing ever seen on this continent. As Shermans army is to march most of the way it will be sometime before the "Grand Review of the Grand Army of the United States" takes place. I hardly think we shall be discharged before fall if we are then   If we are the[re] is many of us think of joining the Regular Service for one year to go on to the borders of Mexico. I have always felt a great interest to see that country and th[ere] is quite a talk of many enlisting for that.

In this you will find a Photgraph of General Emory the Hero and Leader of the old 19th Corps   I must close now as I start for the city soon   Write soon and often   From your True Friend

Abial

May 23rd 1865

Dear Sister [Marcia]

I am so tired   just got in of from the Big Review. I went out with the General. To day has been the greatest day of my life. I rode my horse   It is estimated that 50,000 strangers was here. and such a host of flags mottos etc   To day has repaid me well Marcia for the last 4 years of labor   I will give you a better description at some future time   some of the flags had on them "Welcome Home Brave Boys" "Union Liberty & Freedom the Trio Welcomes their defenders" "All Honor to th[e] Brave who their Country did Save" "We Welcome thee to day our Brave & weep for those who fell our country to Save"   opposite the Treasury was hung out the flag that Booth tore as he jumped from the stage.[1] As we passed the Pres. Platform I saw Grant Sherman, Thomas.[2] The Pres & many others of our noble men. Never shall we see the[ir] like again. It was sad pleasing   sad to think that we had got to be parted   pleasing that we was not needed on the feild of Battle any longer. a Cavalryman gave me a splendid Saber   He belonged to the 6th Penna. Cav. It has been with Sheridans Army in the valley & at Richmond   I wore it to day and shall

send it home at my first opportunity for you to keep for me   To morrow winds up the Greatest Review ever known   after we got in I let
a <u>citz</u> my horse for $5.00   enclosed you will find it. I saw Del Bick-
nere he is in 7th Me Batary   he is comeing over this week to see me.
Love to all

Aff
Abial

1. John Wilkes Booth, Lincoln's assassin, leaped from the presidential box to the
stage at Ford's Theatre, tearing the bunting draped in front of the box.
2. Maj. Gen. George H. Thomas, Sherman's successor as the commander of the
Army of the Tennessee.

Washington DC.
May 26th 1865

My Dear Anna
   Your kind letter of the 22nd is before me & I now hasten to answer
it. Tis a cold rainy day. very disaggreable   This week has been very
buisy with us   Tuesday The Potomac Army our Div & Sherridans
Cavalry was reviewed   It was a spendid day just cool enough to be
pleasant. I went out on the Review with General Beal. As we entered
the city we met the crowd estimated at 50,000 People. Our welcome
will be long remembered and every soldier there felt himself honored
being in that Review. The streets were gaily decorated over the Colums & so was the houses. The First that met us was a banner in-
scribed "Welcome Brave Heroes Welcome Home" The next was.
"The only national debt we never can pay is the debt we owe our
Brave Soldiers['']   But the most interesting was as we came to the
Stage on which the Pres & Lieut Gen Grant sat   I had a good view
of them also General Sherman Gen Thomas Gen Howard[1] Hancock
& numerous others   It was a sight long to be remembered. Th[ere]
was but one thing to mar our pleasure   Th[at] was the thought that
our beloved President A Lincoln should have lived to see this which
his hard work has done for us. Wends the Western Army was Reviewed   I also saw that. It was full as grand as the first days Review   Those who saw it will <u>never forget it</u> <u>never</u>. You ask what I am
doing   not much simply takeing care of the mail. You also ask when
I am comeing home. I think not before fall if we do then as they intend to keep the veterans   I would like much to come home now. For
th[e] war is ended and I want to make my self a home. only think 22
this month (28 May). 4 years more of war would have left me an old
man surely "Grown old before my time"   even now I feel worn out

& much older than I really am but Thank God our hard ships are ended & the Rebels whipped   I regret no hardships that has passed out rather feel proud of it. Many of my friends at these Hed Qurs [Head Quarters] leave for home this next week having served nearly 3 years. It seems hard to part with them I assure you. They are bound to me by nearer ties than could have been formed in civil life   shoulder to shoulder we have stood through all. It seems like seperating with Brothers. God Bless Them & Guard them wherever they are. is my earnest prayer   The Copperheads say the soldiers will come home completely demoralized   I say it is not so. Every good noble feeling has been enlarged while in the army although as they will be very rough yet beneath that rough surface beats hearts so warm & true as never beat beneath the rest of a stay at home fop who would scornfully step aside so that his broadcloth should not come in contact with the army blue (I love that same—blue)   I have often noticed the same thing here in the city of Washington as our poor one armed boys went by. The city gaily dressed and how careful he was not to touch the noble fellow. It would cause me to feel very bitter I assure you Anna. The Army has been a grand school to foster ones best impulses   here he has learned the best & most useful lessons of life & we can go back to a citizens life feeling proud of our position in the years of 61–5. I hope they will let us home this fall but I shall have to wait with patience

Please excuse poor letter Anna & poor wrieting as I came from the city a short time ago & I feel almost numb with the cold. Write soon & often & oblige thy True Friend

Abial H. Edwards
Hd Qs 1st B 1st D 19th C
Washington D.C.

1. Maj. Gen. Oliver O. Howard.

Washington D.C.
May 31st 1865

My Dear Anna

I have some news that dont suit me at all   Our whole Div starts for Savannah Georgia very soon probably this week. Our Orders now is to march at a minutes notice   we shall go by transports   every body feels very bad about it   I think it unjust to us as soldiers. We have staid as long as our country needs us now they ought to discharge us. But the powers that be say nay. Anna please write to me often   We shall be so lonely down there   Oh I dread it more than

words can tell   Please excuse short letter this time for I have a great
deal to do   I will write to you just as soon as we get down there &
write all the news. I will now close this note as I have not time to
write a long letter. Direct to Washington @ 19th A C until you hear
from me again

God Bless You Anna is the Prayers of your
> True Friend
> Abial H Edwards

> On Board Boat. Potomac River
> June 1st 1865

Dear Anna

We are on the boat ready to sail for Savannah early in the morning.
I shall try & send this note so you may know where to direct to. I
want to hear from you <u>often</u> <u>very</u> <u>often</u>   I will write just as soon
as we get there   I think we shall get home some time next fall I
<u>hope</u> <u>so</u> any way. Anna Direct to 1st B- 1st D- 19th A C Savannah
Georgia

No more to night

> Good Bye & sweet dreams
> Aff
> Abial

PART SEVEN

Reconstruction in South Carolina,

1865–1866

INTRODUCTION

Abial Edwards and his regiment became a part of the occupation forces sent south in the immediate aftermath of the war. They left the Potomac on June 1, 1865, and arrived in Savannah after an uneventful voyage, and a few days later were taken to Georgetown, South Carolina. General Beal's brigade, of which the Twenty-ninth Maine was a part, was sent to oversee the military district of eastern South Carolina, that area east of the Wateree River and north of the Santee.

During this period of "presidential reconstruction," the army's purpose was to maintain law and order, settle disputes between the planters and the former slaves, and especially to enforce labor contracts. It worked closely with agents of the Freedmen's Bureau. Morale was low and the duty was boring. The soldiers felt that the war was over and that they had done their part; they wanted to go home. Officers could resign and return to civilian life, but enlisted men could not do that. Many were released because of sickness, however, and gradually enlistments expired and the men returned to Maine. About 14,000 troops were in South Carolina in June 1865, but by January 1866, this number had been halved and by April only approximately 4,500 remained.

Edwards shared the homesickness of his comrades, but he did not share their duties. He became a full-time postmaster, in charge of the mails for the entire military district, a position of great responsibility. Since the Confederate postal system had broken down, and there were no trained postal clerks who would take the loyalty oath, Edwards delivered the mail of the civilian population as well as that of the army. Major Gould, the regimental historian, singles him out for praise. "Corporal Edwards (Co. K), our famous mail agent, by permission of Gen. Beal, undertook the task of carrying and delivering the citizens' mail, as well as that of the army, and succeeded in doing what was in fact a charity to the people, for there was no pay for this increased labor" (591).

While in South Carolina, Edwards developed a real compassion and sympathy for the newly free black citizenry. After watching them celebrate Christmas in 1865, he wrote to Anna: "Truly the negro is a peculiar race & they know far more than we have given them credit for." Not all of the Yankees shared these sentiments. Major Gould, for example, in his regimental history is consistently patronizing and demeaning in his references to "the nigs."

For Edwards, the most important event of his South Carolina tour of duty was the death, in September 1865, of his brother Bela, stationed in Georgetown. Bela was only eighteen months younger than Abial, and the two had been very close. He was devastated with grief. After months of bureaucratic red tape, in early 1866 Edwards was able to bring his brother's body home to Maine for reburial. He remained in Maine on furlough until he was discharged, although he had to go to New York in June to join the remainder of his regiment for the formal mustering out.

BIBLIOGRAPHIC NOTE

The most satisfactory and comprehensive study of reconstruction is Eric Foner, *Reconstruction: America's Unfinished Revolution* 1863–1877 (New York: Harper & Row, 1988). For the army's role, see James E. Sefton, *The United States Army and Reconstruction* 1865–1877 (Baton Rouge: Louisiana State University Press, 1967). The best treatment of South Carolina in this era is Joel Williamson, *After Slavery: The Negro in South Carolina during Reconstruction,* 1861–1877 (Chapel Hill: University of North Carolina Press, 1965). Gould's regimental history, pp. 580–604, covers this period.

> Darlington South Carolina
> Head Quarters. Military District
> Eastern DC
> July 9th 1865

My Dear Anna

I take this my first opportunity for a long while to write you a few lines   as you see we have moved once more. We left Georgetown on the 6th   The General came up on a boat & we came with the troops. I rode horseback in preference to going in the boat. The first days March was very warm & we only [*burned*] miles and at night I told the Generals Private Orderly that if he would start with me that we would go ahead of the troops and so at 9 in the eve we started   we travelled all night   at 12 midnight we reached the Big Black River & as th[ere] was no one to ferry us accross we put our horses on the boat & ferried our selves accross   we broke both poles & liked to have let our selves down the River but we managed to get accross safely. We travelled until 7 in the morning & stoped to a house & found it occupied by a confederate lately returned from the army   he fed our horses and after an hours sleep he gave us a good breakfast & we started on   travelled all day only stopping for dinner and at 4 P.M. of the 7th we had reached Florence 85 miles   you may judge tired we were. Florence is the place where so many of our boys were confined Prisoners & I passed through a grave yard where th[ere] was 4500 buried and th[ere] was another close by that had 5000 buried besides lots that were buried in the woods.[1]

Th[e] men was in a large feild of sand where the burning sun shown down on them all day & they were buried in a sand bed   The way they buried was to dig a trench lay a row of the dead in it face downward pile brush on then & then lay another lot & so on until the trench was full   This is a fact. Th[ere] is a small stone at the head of graves with a number on it   by that means we can tell the exact number buried   The next day after getting into Florence. The General came to this place and established Head Quarters. here it is a pretty little town. Tuesday the cars run direct from Charleston here. Today by the order of the General I was appointed Mail Agent for his whole District embracing several counties   I have to Assistants to help me   I took possession of several mails here & the Post Office. e c belonging to the confederates   I shall go to Charleston once a week my self. It is very sickly here among the Soldiers   several have died within a few days. I dont see no prospect of our getting home for some time yet still we may   We look for a mail to morrow & I shall look for a letter from you. How are you enjoying your self now adays   I suppose that you had a grand time on the 4th of July. I was suffering all [*burned*] with the blues & if I had had wings I should have gone North in a hurry   I will now close   Please write often. for my special interest

> Eer thy Friend
> Abial H. Edwards.
> Mail Agent
> Gen Beals District
> Charleston South Carolina
> via New York

1. The Confederate prisoner-of-war camp at Florence was smaller and less well-known than the one at Andersonville, Georgia. The death rates at these camps were high (34 percent at Salisbury, North Carolina, the worst) because of overcrowding, the lack of supplies and medical facilities, and the breakdown of prisoner-of-war exchanges.

Charleston So. CA.

August 3rd 1865

My Dear Anna

Your thrice welcome missive of the 23rd reached me yesterday and I now take great pleasure in answering it. I have been so very buisy of late that I have neglected writeing to all & I know you would pardon me if you knew the amount of work I have to do. I have all the mail for 9 counties to take care of & you can judge how much it is when I tell you that over 10 villiages have 3000 inhabitants each   The citizens mail & soldiers come to gather   I have now 4 to assist me. but I have to look out for the whole for I I am the only one responsible for any thing. I am here in Charleston now to see about our mail. I will give you an account of this weeks work. Saturday last I came to Charleston. & Monday went back to Darlington giving out 30 mails on the route 114 miles   well I got up there & the General ordered me to visit different places where the confed Post Masters had commenced work & order them to stop it. So I had to start back Tuesday. I shall go back to Darlington to morrow takeing with me 3 large bags of mail which it took me all day yesterday to get ready to deliver & I had 2 to help me. For my part I shall be heartily glad when they do appoint Post Masters. I am about tired out. however I have good accommodations a splendid room here in Charleston & have a team & driver here & in Darlington. I have been so very buisy of late that I have neglected to write to any one So that now I am almost ashamed to commence now. We are having some extremely warm weather now & it is very sickly. Many have died   One of my Mail Carriers is down sick with fever I hardly think he will get well   He was a Noble boy. I miss his help a great deal   It seems sad so many dying out here after the war is ended. Many think that the 29th will be at home in September   I think we shall. I see that Lewiston wants the Reg$^{\perp}$ discharged in that city   I hope not if I go home with the Reg$^{\perp}$ for I once said I never would go to Lewiston again with a company   I prefer to being discharged in Portland instead of going to Lewiston after crackers & salt fish. Dont laugh Anna for I was taken in so once. I will now close but will try & write a more interesting letter soon   Write often Direct as before

From Thy Friend
Abial. H. Edwards.
Head Quarters
Gen Beals Brigade
Charleston So Ca

Headquarters Military District
Eastern S. C.
Third Separate Brigade
Darlington, S. C.
August 13th 1865

My Dear Sister [Marcia]

Having some leisure time to day I thought I would improve it in writing to you. Sundays here are the longest days we have. and we have to contrive to pass away time the best way we can. You recollect that miniture of Negro Jim I sent you last winter   well he died this morning   Poisened to death he says. He was a faithful servant & I think a good christian. Now I do not regret at all the time I passed last winter in reading the Bible to him   he used to come in quite often & get me to read it for him. I hope he is better of. The longer I live in the South the more I hate this "Divine Institution" Slavery. It is the greatest curse america has ever had. I have talked with many negroes & asked them what Freedom meant   they must all have a good idea of it. One big fellow some over 6 ft I asked and he straitened up & said "it meant he was now a man"   The Negroes Love for "Yankees" is great. We got some to clean out the Court House for us & one asked for pay   another stepped up to the first & said what ask these <u>genniman</u> for pay when they have worked for us for the last 4 years   he fairly shamed the other out of it. Still I dont beleive in the Negroes voting right away   they aint as yet capable of it   they have got to have their minds grow with their freedom   now they are to easily influenced & it would be by this means that the Southern <u>gentleman</u> would get the power into their own hands. I should fight against their voteing & we let them be content with what has been given them & wait patiently for the rest which in time will come round all right   Dont you say so. The Rebels some of them yet show a bad temper   They have tried to burn the New Era Office & I shouldnt be surprised if they tried the "Yanke Post Office" yet. The

Era Office is on the Opposite side of the street from me. I dont have much to do with the citizens here   Nothing more than what is necessary. They aint to be trusted yet. Well those boys from my Reg᛫ start for home next Tuesday. We are glad for them yet we shall miss them a great deal. As I am writeing we are having a fine shower. Most every body thinks that troops will be kept here until the crops are divided among the freedmen & owners to see that it is done fair   That will take some time yet but I shall be contented as long as my health is good. Well no more now. Love to Clestice & all the rest. I have ordered a box made for the saddle. McLellan Saddle Gov Price $28.00   worth keeping aint it   I shall forward it soon

Aff Brother Abial

Headquarters Military
District, S.C.
Third Separate Brigade.
Darlington, S.C.,
Sept. 12th 1865

My Dear Friend

  Your kind favor of Aug 24th was received last night & I now hasten to answer it. I was much pleased to hear from you. As for my self I never was quite so buisy all the time Since I was in the army as I now am. I have charge of all mails from Charleston, So. Ca. to Wilmington, N.C. I have 12 mail carriers on the route. I have to go to Florence daily to receipt for the mails. Florence is 12 miles from here. I have a car & engine to take me down so I go in a very short time. I also have charge of this Post Office yet. I like the work still it is very confined life   I was in hope that the 29th was going home soon but am disappointed in that as they have commenced giving out furloughs 25 for every 100 men. & it appears by that that we shall stop out here this winter. I think very strongly of having a furlough next month (Oct) if I can get away   the furloughs are for 30 days. I have hardly decided yet however. If you could only be here now to enjoy the Splendid Peaches Grapes & all the fruits that grow so plentifully in the "Sunny South" I know you would enjoy it. But I think I should enjoy a visit North now very much   I think if I allowed my self to think seriously of it that I should be tempted to go North. My Brother is still very ill & I am real anxious about him   I am in hopes to get him home on a furlough for I think he will not recover if he stops here in this climate. If I can get him a furlough I think I had better be contented & stay here my self   I see the 30th Maine has got home   I am glad for them still I should be more pleased if they would take interest enough in the 29th to let that Reg⊥ see the state once more. I am ashamed to write to any one lately   we have no news to write worth writting & I hardly know how to begin a letter. Please excuse all errors & bad writeing. Excuse haste for I want to get this out in the afternoon mail. I send a mail to Charleston & Wilmington daily   Write soon & often & Oblige Your Friend

Abial. H. Edwards.

[Penciled note at end of letter, presumably written by Anna:]
Only "your friend Abial" very evident that there is not interest enough on the part of the writer of this to warrant the continuance of this correspondence   long as it has been kept up it has lost interest rather than gained.

Darlington   H. So Ca
Sept 15th 1865

My Dear Anna
   Tis midnights quiet hour but sleep is not for me   I have lost my only relative that was out here. My Dear Brother Died the 3rd of this month at Georgetown So Ca only 85 miles from me but he died so suddenly that I could not see him   he has been sick with fever & he wrote to me the 25 of Aug that he was gaining fast. but as his Capt wrote to me he was suddenly taken with cancer in the throat which proved fatel in a short time. It's very hard for me to bear. I can not be reconciled to my loss. I have loved my country as few has loved it yet this is a sacrifice I little dreamed of. My Brother was 20 years of age being only 18 months younger than myself & since we have been out here we have depended a good deal upon each others company. I am now alone. It seems hard to me to know I was so near yet knew not his fatel sickness until all was over. I feel rebellious. I cant help it. My cry is Oh Lord why is it So. Why have I always been afflicted while others have moved quietly on the stream of life. The surface not even ruffled for them. My whole life has been centered in my Brothers & Sisters. Little did I think this war was to strike me so near   How I long to fly that I might help concole the Dear ones at home   But it is my lot to suffer alone. Not with out friends however for many have called that are true & sympathizing friends. Chaplain Whita-more Editor of New Era Major Gould & the General all have helped me to meet my trial. But they are not the relatives at home that feel

as I feel in our deep affliction. But Anna I do not feel like writing to night therefore you must excuse me. Please write soon

> To Your True Friend
> Abial H. Edwards.
> Gen Beals HeadQuarters
> via Charleston So Ca

> Darlington Post Office
> Sept 30th 1865

My Dear Anna

I have not felt like writing to any one in the last few gloomy weeks. It has been a hard blow to me to lose my Brother here. I have made preperations to go to Maine with My Brothers Remains in November   it will be a sad sad task but I can not see him laid away in this state & if I live 2 months from now will find his body beside our Mother & Sisters in the quiet church yard at home   It is my duty to do so. Oh Anna it seems as though I have had nothing but bitter lessons in this life. I am tired & weary of it   I feel thankful that I have so much work to do to keep my mind buisy   Write soon   The Mail is now ready to leave. I will write soon again

> Thy Friend
> Abial

1. Abial's mother, Dorcas Caswell Whitney Edwards, died Dec. 14, 1855. His sister, Maria Louise, died March 3, 1856.

> Headquarters Military District
> Eastern S.C.
> Third Separate Brigade
> Darlington, S.C.
> Oct 18th 1865.

My Dear Friend Anna

Your very kind favor was received last night & I now hasten to answer it. I had hoped ere this to be on my way North with my Brothers Remains but was disappointed as I cant until Dec. I tell you Anna this has been a gloomy place to me for the last month. Were it not for a plenty of work I dont know what I should have done   as it is time drags heavily. When I look back & see how hard I tried to keep my brother out of service & now to think we never shall meet again. Gone forever I can not realize it. Would that I had the Spirit to say. "Thy will not mine be done" The 15th Maine is to be removed from that dredful place Georgetown & brought up here over 60 of the Reg' has died there. As yet I see no prospect of our getting out of service this fall I think we shall have to remain until Spring. Colonel Nye is now at home on furlough he will be back. About one fourth of the 29th is at home on furlough I am very sorry to hear you had been ill. I hope to hear that you are enjoying the best of health next time you write. Do you think of stopping in Lewiston this winter. I dislike the sound of that place I hardly know why. It is begining to be quite cool here nights so one needs his overcoat on The[re] is a great many of our Reg' that has gone to Lewiston on furlough. If you could only be here this morning & enjoy the rich notes of the mocking bird I know it would please you they are very thick about here & we can hear them at all hours of the day. Gen Beal is still here & I think will remain until we all go home he is liked very much by all citizens & soldiers as well. I havent much news to write this time. Please excuse this poorly written scrawl. Write often for I dont know what I would do were it not for my letters.

Hopeing to hear from you
soon I Remain Your True Friend
Abial H Edwards
Gen Beals Hd Quarters
Darlington So. Ca
via Wilmington N.C.

Headquarters Military District
Eastern S.C.
Third Separate Brigade
Darlington, S.C.
Oct 22nd 1865

My Dear Anna

I will try & write you a few lines to day. but at first I will say they will be very uninteresting. Of late it has been an effort for me to write at all. As I sat this morning listning to the music of the Church bells It carried me back to years gone by. to the time when my brother & I were sent to church & Sabbath School with a fond Mothers Kiss. but now how changed. Mother & Brother gone before. Every thing recalls the lost ones. But our loss is their gain. The trials of this world will trouble them no more. I was in hopes to come home this month with my Brothers remains but I find out that I can not until December. Then I shall go if nothing happens. I see no prospect of our getting home to Stay before Spring. I think I should feel much better if I was free & at the North as it is I must try & be contented as I can here. Autumn has already began to paint nature in the bright colors of the rainbow. & the mocking birds are very numerous. giving us their rich & varied music so that we could imagine all kinds of Birds were singing instead of one. But you know the old saying, "Home is where the heart is" & I beleive it. for with all the beauties of the south. I much prefer the north & true friends there than the distant & reserved Southerners who have a holy horror of & perfectly detest the "Low born Yankees." While Gov is keeping us here the President is fast yeilding inch by inch all we have gained in our years of toil & strife & the very worst that were are fighting against.[1] are having all the rights of citizenship accorded to them that they may once more turn against the old victorious Red White & Blue. I think my self it is best to be magnanimous to our conquired foe. But not so much so that a few years hence that the serpent (Traitors) will once more become gigantic in size. & cause us all the sorrows of the last few years. God knows I want to see no more of such Strife such costly sacrafices. as we have given to the alter of Liberty. We should only love our country the more & guard it the more sacredly. from its once powerful foe. Still time may show my ideas are all wrong. I hope so. To day is warm & mild as mid summer. Nights however are very chilly. I shall direct this to Canton as presume you are still there I would like to hear from you as often as possible for I hardly know what I should do were it not for my letters I have many friends who were with me in the campaign last summer & who are now at home that write often to me. By this I manage to help drive a part of the Blues away. Excuse all errors & write often

Thy Friend Abial
Gen Beals Head Quarters
Darlington C. H. So CA
via Wilmington N.C.

1. He is referring to President Andrew Johnson's mild treatment of the South, and especially his pardons of thousands of former Confederates.

Darlington Post Office So. Ca
Nov 10th 1865

My Dear Friend

I will endeavor to write you a few lines to day although of late it is a great effort for me to write at all. Tis a fine pleasant day. almost like summer   still I long for the cold North   my heart is there with the friends I have been so long seperated from   As times rolls slowly on I miss my Brother more & more. Sometimes I can hardly contain my self & I have to leave the cheerful company in my room & take a long walk alone to clear my troubled mind. & in the still quiet evening my thoughts goes out to that little mound near the fever swamps of Georgetown. which is all that is left here to show I had once a Brother here with me. In all my soldiers life through all the heart rending scenes I have passed nothing can compare with this. To think my Brother travelled down to the shores of the Dark River with out the hand of a relative being near to help his tedious sick hours. I have one consolation allowed me. Sept 3rd the day he died th[ere] was another one near him who was to leave the shores of time. He died the same time by the side of My Brother & as the Hospital Steward informs me, he died a fearful death. My Brother suffered fearfully all day but not a groan not a murmer escaped him. The Steward asked him if he had any word or message to leave. He roused up & said he had. He said Give all my effects to Brother Abial. & tell him he knows my wishes in regard to my property. Tell him <u>all is well</u>   This was the last. he fell asleep never more to be awakened on the shores of time. When the time draws near, when "all is well" with us then we can be reunited in a better land. A few weeks ago I understood that a cousin of mine in Portland was to be married & I sent her a pair of white kids for a wedding gift   her letter that answered mine told me of the death of her intended one whom she idolized & loved more than life itself. Truly I am not alone in my sorrow. You must excuse me Anna   I do not feel like writeing a cheerful letter & I know you would not want any other. I presume by this time you are in Lewiston & having a plenty of snow. Please write soon. It is nearly time for the mail to leave & I will now close

Thy Friend
Abial H. Edwards
Head Quarters
Military District
Eastern South Carolina
Darlington C So CA

December 1st 1865

My Dear Sister [Marcia]
It has been quite a while since I wrote a letter because in fact I had <u>just</u> <u>nothing</u> to write. Well I must tell you a few weeks ago I got an

Autograph Album and commenced gettting persons to write their
names in it. Well last night Gen. U. S. Grant came through Florence
and stoped there an hour and shook hands with soldiers all around.
After an introduction to him by Capt. Pray[1] I asked him if he would
give me his name in my album, certainly he said if he only had the
materials. I took this gold pen out of my pocket and some ink and he
wrote his name in my Book. <u>Bully</u> <u>for</u> <u>that</u>. The officers none of them
thought of taking their albums so they could get names too (for my
getting one made them all the rage) and they all envy me mine. Lt.
Stacy[2] said he would give me $25.00) I could easily get $50.00 just
because Grant's name is in it. I am going to fill it up and send it
home.[3] among those who have already been here and wrote their
names is General Beal, Gen. Howard, Gen. Nye,[4] Gen Richardson,
Lieut Gen Grant and lots of lesser officers. I wouldn't take $10,000
in gold for it would you. The[re] is no news to write. I am looking
anxiously for the Pay Mestir then I will let you know when I can come
home.

Love to all
Aff Brother
Abial

1. Capt. Almon Clark Pray of Company I.
2. Brvt. 1st Lt. Lorenzo D. Stacy from Porter, Maine.
3. The autograph album and gold pen are still preserved with the letters and
other family papers (see photo 18). As well as the names mentioned, it includes
autographs of C. B. Fillebrown, John Gould, Henry Kallock, and Artemus Ward
(Charles F. Browne), humorous writer and lecturer.
4. Col. George H. Nye, the regimental commander, was breveted as a brigadier
general in October 1865.

Head Quarters
3rd Seperate Brig
Darlington Court House S.C.
Dec 21st 1865

My Dear Friend
   Your kind letter reached me last night   it was thrice welcome &
read with much pleasure   We are having some very pleasant weather
now. just cool enough to be comfortable & aggreeable. I have been to
Charleston this week got back last night feeling much better for my
trip. I do really beleive if I had not so much to do & look out for I
should die of the blues. As it is I find it very hard to feel as I should.
I started for Charleston Monday night & on our way down about 3 in

the morning (Tuesday) as the train was going quite fast every wheel run out from under the Passenger car. & let the car down on the track. I got slightly hurt. lamed my arm & side but I feel better to night no one was seriously injured. It was a very fortunate escape for us all. On my way back I had company Major General Saxton[1] & 3 of his staff. He talked with me for some time I found him a very pleasant gentleman. He will be up here to morrow. General Nye has been gone some time but got back to day. The 15th Maine is to leave this District altogather & is to be sent into the Western District South Carolina. Thus you see instead of discharging any Reg⊥s they prefer to scatter them around the State. Officers & men have all come to the conclusion that we have got to remain here all winter & therefore the[re] isnt much said about going home. The Major advise me to go home in January & I think I shall I dislike to delay going home but he thinks I had better wait for several reasons. I dread it so much & still I want to go & must go. My folks seem to think that I must not come back here & I know very well I must therefore I dread to go on my sad journey. I beleive th[ere] is several that belongs to my Company still in Lewiston on furlough. I suppose they are dreading to leave home. but I see not the least promise of our going home & being mustered out until spring & perhaps late at that. However it is best to be contented & in time we shall become private citizens once more. Some of the "boys" that have been home on furlough come back with a very poor opinion of the people of the North they tell me that if a Soldier goes into any place of amusement dressed in uniform & take a seat near a Lady that she will instantly leave the seat. However I told them that would not disturbe me as I should remain away from such places & give them no chance for such slights I have worn my countrys blue too long to be ashamed of it. It has been my lot to be one who has given one of my dearest relatives for my countrys good yes I have no cause to blame my country for that I feel it to become dearer to me for that reason In the lone quiet nights when alone I often awake & think of the past at such times I feel alone in every meaning of the word then my loss comes to me with such a force that I long for some one to be near that will cause such a feeling to leave me. After I received news of my Brothers Death It worried me so much to think it was not my privilage to be there with him that for nights in my dreams I witnessed the terrible scenes of his Death Bed. I have reason to be thankful that my Sisters do not know the scenes or trials of a Hospital for if they had seen so many die with no friends near & still heer them calling so earnistly for them as I have they would feel as I do about it. But I hope they

will never know the scenes of such a place. I fear however I am tireing
you Anna & giving you a very poor letter in return for yours. Please
write soon & often.

> Thy Friend
> Abial H. Edwards
> Mail Off
> Gen Richardson Head Quarters
> Darlington South Carolina
> via Wilmington N.C.

1. Maj. Gen. Rufus B. Saxton, a Maine native, had been in South Carolina since
the Union occupation of the coastal areas in 1862 and was especially concerned
about the welfare of the black population.

Christmas. 1865

My Dear Friend

I take pen in hand to write you a few lines   I hardly know what
for you know my inability to write a letter fit for one to read. Tis
Christmas Eve the day has been very warm & pleasant & the colored
population has been swarming into town by the hundreds. & every
avaliable place has been taken for their uncouth & weird dances &
such music as they have   reeds violins Banjos & everything one could
think of that is capable of makeing music   some is truly comic &
laughable while others is so very sad that it affects the hearer with a
gloomy meaning. Truly the negro is a peculiar race & they know far
more than we have given them credit for. perhaps so much as our race
could have known had we been under the same bond of slavery.
Thank God the shackels are broken & our country will never more
know the curse of Slavery. Last night I had to sit up until 12 at night
for the mail & it brought to mind the many times I have watched for
the comeing of "Santa Claus" & his good faries with the dear Brothers
& Sisters at home. (Happy days of childhood   how my heart cries
out for the past joys never more to come again)   Little did I think
when my school days seemed so irksome that they were my happiest
days. How I would like the perfect happiness of such days to return   I think I could appreciate it fully. And now Anna how has
Christmas passed with thy self. I have thought you might be at home
with the family circle or perhaps at Lewiston. Where ever you may be
I hope you may enjoy your self better than I have. How often may the
old saying prove true   a smileing countenance may hide a tired ach-

ing heart. Let one enjoy themselves as best they can. Olden memories will come unbidden & silence the pleasures of the present   Thanksgiving & Christmas has come & gone. with out little pleasure on my part. Far from the family circle that met at home last January there is now a vacent chair. America with all her anthems & shouts of Peace has many acheing hearts. How thankful I have been Anna that you have been blessed as you have no kindred have you been obliged to give up in this struggle. To day has been very warm & pleasant so that I have had doors & windows open all day. & even now 8 P.M. I am sitting with doors open. How I wish that we could have such mild winters in Old Maine   Anna I think you will find this a dull letter   better still I know you will pardon me for Christmas is a poor day for writing letters. Excuse all errors & write soon   I sent you a few of "Petterson's"[1] for I hope they may prove acceptable. The[re] is many interesting peices in them. I will now close. Please write soon & accept this poor apology of a letter from

> Thy True Friend
> Abial H. Edwards.
> Co K 29th Me
> Darlington So Ca

PS. As you will get this about the 1st Jan/66 I wish you a <u>Happy New Year</u>

> Abial
> via Wilmington.

1. *Peterson's Magazine* was a popular illustrated magazine for women.

> Florence S.C.
> Military Post Office.
> 3d Seperate Brigade
> Jan 5th 1866

My Dear Anna

Your thrice welcome letter reached me. A few days ago but as I was very buisy in moving I could not answer before this. Gen Richardson gave me orders to move my office to this place & take all my mail messengers with me. We are now 12 miles from Darlington. Here the[re] is 3 Rail Roads connect & as all mails come here it was necessary for me to be here. There is 5 mails a day comeing in here & it gives me more work than ever. Some nights I have between 30 & 40 bags of mail to look out for. besides a great deal of loose mail to distribute around. I am glad to get more work. Time passes away much quicker for me. Florence you recollect is the place where so many of the "boys in blue" gave up their lives in the Prison Pen. The stockade is about a mile from my place   I have been all through it. I wish you could look at it & then you could have a faint idea of the Poor Fellows suffering. To day I will send you a book the title of it is "Nameless"   all I shall say about it is I <u>like it</u> & I hope you will. We have had extremely chill weather for a number of days but this morning the sun is Shineing right pleasantly. Give me the pleasant winters of the South & the summers of the North. Some of the 29th whose time is out is to be discharged this month. One of them got married this week to a Southern Lady & several of them are going to remain & settle out here. It looks very singular to me that so many of the girls of the south should mary yankees after being so bitter against them. Now you cant take up a paper of South Carolina but what you can see the marriage of some of them with the Yankee Soldiers stationed in this state. Th[ere] was a Chaplain sent out to the 29th got here last night. The question now is when is the 29th to be discharged   I say give me active service in preference to helping reconstruct South Carolina   Anna I think you will say. Dont send any more such dry epistles but the fact is I have nothing to write worth writeing. Still you must take the will for the deed. Capt Kingsley intends to resign soon & go home. I beleive. I will now close. Write soon & often from your True Friend

> Abial H Edwards.
> Gen Richardsons Head Quarters
> Florence S.C.
> via Wilmington N.C.

> Portland Maine
> April 25th 1866

Friend Anna

   I hardly know how to commence or what to say in this letter. I dont know what has caused this long silence. I came home over 2 months ago & about 6 weeks before I started I got no letters that were sent to me   I think they were all destroyed through malice by one of my mail carriers that I sent to his company for getting drunk. However I wrote to you telling you I was comeing with my Brothers Remains & for you to write to Casco to me   when I got there th[ere] was no letter for me. After the funeral & after I had rested (for I was all tired out & nearly sick) I went to Portland and from there to Lewiston. About 5 days before I went I wrote to you telling you what day I was to be there. & for you to leave a note letting me know where you boarded   I went there & found no note for me & a friend of mine said he knew a Miss Conant by sight & that he knew a fellow paying the lady attention but he had not seen Miss Conant lately & thought she was out of town   he described Miss Conant & I thought by the Description it was you & thought your silence was for me to cease the correspondence   Anna is it so   if it is please let me know for I had much rather have it from your own lips than from silence. I was very sorry it hapened so   the day I went to Lewiston I took a great lot of either [ether] & had some teeth extracted & I was so under the in-fluance of it that I slept all the way up after being out all evening   my friends made me go into the Hall with them & it af-fected me so I fainted & had to be helped out   the next day I was taken quite ill & fearing I was to be worse I came right back home. I am out of the service as I came home on furlough & went to see the Governor & he sent for my Discharge   I am going to open a store here next week. Please write me one line if no more so that this anx-iety will be done away with. If you are not in Lewiston perhaps some of your friends will send this to you. I hope so. I will not trouble you to much to day until I hear from you. Please write one line if no more

As ever your Friend
Abial H. Edwards.
Portland Maine
Box 388.

Portland
June 30th 1866

My Dear Anna

Your welcome missive I received yesterday & was pleased to hear from you   I was very sorry to hear of your leaving Lewiston as you did so soon. I had got ready to leave & was going to Lewiston on Monday noon train when I got your letter stating that you was going to leave the day you wrote so I gave up going to that place. I am in hopes to meet you there when you return from Canton [Maine]   I have been to New York & met the 29th Maine & got mustered out of service   I got back here yesterday & feel quite tired to day. I hope I have not got to travel any more for a long while for to me it is very tiresome. I shall send you some papers to read occasionally. It must be very quiet to you in the country now. I have been in the Army so long

that I dont think I should feel contented in a quiet place   My Part-
ner's health is very poor & I think we shall sell out & I hardly know
where I shall go probably stay here & in Lewiston
     Please let me hear from you soon

Your True Friend
A. H. Edwards
Box 388

Afterword

There are many more letters to Anna from Abial in the years following the war. The transition to civilian life was not easy. Abial's first business venture, in which he had invested his wartime savings, was lost in a Portland fire in 1866. He then worked in the Customs House in Portland, separating imports by destination, and there he attended business college.

Remaining are letters detailing his continued and somewhat stormy courtship of Anna, as she began to question his intentions. In 1868 he freed her from her promises because of his inability to support her, explaining the deathbed promise he had made to his mother to see his younger siblings established in life. To this end, he was still helping his younger brother Philip, and paying part of the boarding bills for his two younger sisters, Josie and Kate, in order that they might complete their high school education. The correspondence lapsed for a short time, and then resumed.

Abial and Anna seldom saw each other due to distance and the hours of Abial's work. He had no holidays. There are intimations that Anna saw other men, perhaps to stir Abial to action, but his letters are gently persistent. One should not forget how young both of them were when the correspondence began. At age twenty-six Abial finally decided that he was ready to take on the responsibilities of a family. He and Anna were married in Portland on October 18, 1869, and moved into a boarding house there. During the next seven years they lived in several rented homes in Lynn and Chelsea, Massachusetts, before moving to Casco in 1877, where Abial died at age thirty-four. His youngest child, Ethel May, died in the same year at the age of fourteen months. Both are buried beside Abial's parents Samuel and Dorcas, his brother Bela, and his sisters Maria and Josie in the Green Grove Cemetery in Casco.

During their marriage Anna, and later the children, were sent "home" each summer, as was the custom, to protect them from the heat and disease of the city. Their daughter Edith spent time with

Abial's sister, Marcia, who had married Jordan Cook, in Casco, while Anna visited her family in Canton. Abial wrote faithfully and affectionately to both of them describing his work, his illnesses, his loneliness, and his domestic efforts to ready the house for their return.

Later letters provide information about Abial's younger sisters. Josie became engaged to Frank Martin. No marriage is mentioned, and she died at age twenty-four. Katie married Frank Littlefield in 1876, who drowned in a tragic boating accident a few months later. She remarried in 1877, to Frank Carter.

Anna remarried in 1898. (She commented in a diary how she continued to miss Abial.) Her two children, Philip and Edith, were then grown. Edith, who inherited her father's penchant for writing letters, corresponded regularly with her mother. Through these letters we learn of her brother Philip's marriage to Chestina Marsh, and about his early business experiences before becoming a sporting goods salesman.

Edith had a very stormy courtship of her own with George Hayes, similar to that of her parents, although their separations were caused not by war but by the dislocations of unemployment arising from the industrial depression, as George followed job leads up and down the East coast. They too eventually overcame these problems, and were married in Strong, Maine, in 1893. Again Edith's life paralleled her father's, when she died in 1902 at age thirty-two, leaving a young child, Dorothy, and an infant, Philip, named after his uncle. A very moving letter to Anna from Marcia describes the family's grief.

Anna attempted to raise her grandchildren, but became ill and died in 1905 in Lawrence, Massachusetts, at age 63, of what was probably a ruptured appendix. Dorothy and Philip Hayes were boarded out to distant relatives and friends on the paternal Hayes side, and contact with the Edwards family was lost for about seventy years.

In 1970 Beverly Hayes Kallgren, daughter of Philip Hayes, vacationed in Rangeley, Maine. In describing her itinerary to her father she mentioned the town of Wilton, and he remembered having a cousin there whom he had not seen since early childhood. On her next trip to Maine she located the cousin, Robert Edwards. He showed her a collection of old family letters he had found in the barn of his mother's home in Dixfield, Maine, following her death. It was she, Chestina Marsh, Abial's daughter-in-law, who was responsible for saving the letters.

Philip Hayes not only enjoyed reading the Civil War letters of his grandfather, but he learned previously unknown facts about his family history from later letters written to Anna by his parents, Edith Edwards and George Hayes.

In 1974 the two cousins, Philip Hayes, son of Edith Edwards Hayes, and Robert Edwards, son of Philip Waldo Edwards, were reunited. They found many common interests other than the letters and their mutual grandparents, and they enjoyed several years of warm friendship before Philip's death in 1985.

The letters were then turned over to Beverly Hayes Kallgren. The result is this book.

Appendix:
Edwards Family Genealogy

1. John Edwards   b. 168-
   d. 3/16/1757
   married: Lydia Crockett 11/1712 Portsmouth, N.H.
   b. 1683
   d. ?
   children: <u>John</u>   b. 11/10/1713 Haverhill, Mass.
   d. 3/6/1756 Haverhill, Mass.
   Nathaniel   b. 3/14/1715 Haverhill, Mass.
   d. ?

2. John Edwards occ: cooper
   married: Elizabeth Crockett 12/15/1737 Haverhill, Mass.
   b. ?
   d. ?
   children: John   b. 10/28/1738 Haverhill, Mass.
   d. 1789
   Richard   b. 9/5/1740 Haverhill, Mass.
   d. 10/29/1826 Gorham, Me.
   Susanna   b. 4/12/1743 Haverhill, Mass.
   d. 4/12/1743 Haverhill, Mass.
   Rachel   b. 4/12/1743 Haverhill, Mass.
   d. 4/12/1743 Haverhill, Mass.
   Elizabeth   b. 6/23/1744 Haverhill, Mass.
   d. 1/5/1748-9 Haverhill, Mass.
   Jonathan   b. 3/28/1747 Haverhill, Mass.
   d. 10/30/1837 Otisfield, Me.
   Samuel   b. 2/16/1749 Haverhill, Mass.
   d. ?

	Nathaniel	b. 6/21/1752 Haverhill, Mass.
		d. 6/14/1828 Otisfield, Me.
	William	b. 4/27/1755 Haverhill, Mass.
		d. 12/15/1845 Otisfield, Me.

3. Nathaniel Edwards occ: farmer
married: Sarah Hunt 10/1775 Gorham, Me.

		b. 4/10/1754
		d. 3/5/1832 Casco, Me.
children:	George	b. 8/3/1776 Gorham, Me.
		d. 9/30/1847 Casco, Me.
	John	b. 10/3/1777 Gorham, Me.
		d. 11/3/1849 Casco, Me.
	William	b. 6/11/1793 Casco, Me.
		d. ? Ohio
	Nathaniel	b. 5/24/1795 Casco, Me.
		d. 1846 Gardiner, Me.
	Sarah	b. 7/31/1781 Casco, Me.
		d. 7/28/1855 Raymond, Me.
	Mary	b. 5/20/1784 Casco, Me.
		d. 1/4/1863 Otisfield, Me.
	Hannah	b. 12/29/1784 Casco, Me.
		d. 5/10/1867 Peru, Me.
	Elizabeth	b. 2/27/1789 Casco, Me.
		d. 12/14/1865
	Lucy P.	b. 7/11/1791 Casco, Me.
		d. 4/1866 Casco, Me.
	Susannah	b. 7/17/1800 Casco, Me.
		d. 1865 Turner, Me.

4. John Edwards occ: farmer
married: Susanna Scribner

		b. 1788 Otisfield, Me.
		d. ?
children:	Samuel Goodale	b. 1/28/1809 Otisfield, Me.
		d. 12/22/1883 Casco, Me.
	Bela Cass	b. 8/29/1812 Casco, Me.
		d. 1870 at sea
	Daniel	b. 8/29/1814 Casco, Me.
		d. 10/22/1859 Casco, Me.
	Luther	b. 11/28/1816 Casco, Me.
		d. 4/16/1875 Casco, Me.
	Susan Mehittable	b. 6/1821 Casco, Me.
		d. 6/27/1855 Casco, Me.

5. Samuel Goodale Edwards occ: wheelwright, carriage maker
    married: Dorcas Caswell Whitney 12/14/1837

	b. 10/20/1820
	d. 10/8/1855
children: Susan Marcia	b. 3/8/1840 Casco, Me.
	d. ?
Samuel	b. 3/7/1842 Casco, Me.
	d. 3/7/1842 Casco, Me.
John	b. 3/7/1842 Casco, Me.
	d. 3/15/1842 Casco, Me.
Abial Hall Scribner	b. 5/28/1843 Casco, Me.
	d. 10/15/1877 Casco, Me.
Bela	b. 2/3/1845 Harrison, Me.
	d. 9/3/1865 Georgetown, S.C.
Philip Wadleigh	b. 7/4/1848 Raymond, Me.
	d. 4/10/1873 Boston, Mass.
Josephine	b. 8/14/1850 Casco, Me.
	d. 9/11/1874 Casco, Me.
Maria Louise	b. 8/14/1850 Casco, Me.
	d. 3/5/1856 Casco, Me.
Hadassah Kate	b. 3/22/1853 Casco, Me.
	d. ?

6. ABIAL HALL SCRIBNER EDWARDS occ: merchant, postal worker
    married: Anna Lucinda Conant 10/18/1869 Portland, Me.

	b. 11/4/1843 Canton, Me.
	d. 9/1/1905 Lawrence, Mass.
children: Edith Josephine	b. 9/25/1870 Chelsea, Mass.
	d. 12/8/1902 Lawrence, Mass.
Philip Waldo	b. 6/14/1873 Chelsea, Mass.
	d. 10/21/1909 Portland, Me.
Ethel May	b. 8/14/1876 Canton, Me.
	d. 10/22/1877 Casco, Me.

DESCENDANTS

7. Edith Josephine Edwards occ: musician and housewife
    married: George Edward Hayes 8/14/1893 Strong, Me.

	b. 11/25/1870 Newfield, Me.
	d. 1939 Boston, Mass.
children: Dorothy Edwards	b. 7/17/1895 Greenville, N.H.
	d. 6/23/1927 Saranac Lake, N.Y.

<u>Philip Raymond</u>   b. 5/5/1901 Lawrence, Mass.

                             d. 12/23/1985 Torrington, Conn.

Philip Waldo Edwards
married: Chestina Marsh 6/9/1899 Dixfield, Me.

                             b. 7/27/1875

                             d. 5/17/1958

children: Robert Marsh   b. 4/14/1903

                             d.

      Margaret Hope   b. 9/14/1909

                             d. 1/5/1966

8. Philip Raymond Hayes occ: insurance executive
married: Mabel Suphronia Long 6/18/1923 Allston, Mass.

                             b. 1/18/1901 Boston, Mass.

                             d.

children: Beverly Arleen   b. 5/10/1925 Boston, Mass.

                             d.

[1]Information preceding 1915 from *A Genealogical Record of the Descendants of John Edwards 168– to 1915* by Llewellyn Nathanial Edwards. Bangor, Maine: Thomas W. Burr Printing & Adv. Co., 1916. Information after 1915 from Kallgren, Hayes, and Edwards family records.

Bibliography

Barton, Michael. *Goodmen: The Character of Civil War Soldiers.* University Park: Pennsylvania State University Press, 1981.

Carter, Robert Goldthwaite. *Four Brothers in Blue.* 1913. Reprint. Austin: University of Texas Press, 1978.

Davis, William C., ed. *The Image of War 1861–1865.* 6 vols. Garden City, N.Y.: Doubleday and Co., 1981–84.

Donald, David Herbert, ed. *Gone for A Soldier: The Civil War Memoirs of Private Alfred Bellard.* Boston: Little, Brown, 1975.

Foner, Eric. *Reconstruction: American's Unfinished Revolution 1863–1877.* New York: Harper & Row, 1988.

Foote, Shelby. *The Civil War: A Narrative.* 3 vols. New York: Random House, 1958–74.

Geary, James W. *We Need Men: The Union Draft in the Civil War.* DeKalb: Northern Illinois University Press, 1991.

Gould, John M. *History of the First-Tenth-Twenty-ninth Maine Regiment.* Portland: Stephen Berry, 1870.

Harrington, Fred Harvey. *Fighting Politician: Major General N. P. Banks.* Philadelphia: University of Pennsylvania Press, 1948.

Hess, Earl J., ed. *A German in The Yankee Fatherland: The Civil War Letters of Henry A. Kircher.* Kent, Ohio: Kent State University Press, 1983.

Johnson, Ludwell H. *Red River Campaign: Politics and Cotton in the Civil War.* Baltimore: The Johns Hopkins University Press, 1958.

Kohl, Lawrence Frederick, and Margaret Coose Richard, eds. *Irish Green and Union Blue: The Civil War Letters of Peter Welsh.* New York: Fordham University Press, 1986.

Linderman, Gerald F. *Embattled Courage: The Experience of Combat in the American Civil War.* New York: The Free Press, 1987.

Livermore, Thomas L. *Battles and Losses in the Civil War in America 1861–1865.* Boston and New York: Houghton Mifflin Co., 1901.

McPherson, James M. *Battle Cry of Freedom: The Civil War Era.* New York: Oxford University Press, 1988.

Merrill, George Drew, ed. *History of Androscoggin County, Maine.* Boston: W. A. Ferguson & Co., 1891.

Mitchell, Reid. *Civil War Soldiers.* New York: Viking Press, 1988.

Murdock, Eugene C. *One Million Men: The Civil War Draft in the North.* Madison: State Historical Society of Wisconsin, 1971.

Nevins, Allan. *The War for the Union.* 4 vols. New York: Charles Scribner's Sons, 1959–71.

Rhodes, Robert Hunt, ed. *All for the Union: The Civil War Diary and Letters of Elisha Hunt Rhodes.* 1985. Reprint. New York: Orion Books, 1991.

Robertson, James I., Jr. *Soldiers Blue and Gray.* Columbia: University of South Carolina Press, 1988.

Sears, Stephen W. *Landscape Turned Red: The Battle of Antietam.* New Haven and New York: Ticknor and Fields, 1983.

Sefton, James E. *The United States Army and Reconstruction 1865–1877.* Baton Rouge: Louisiana State University Press, 1967.

Shannon, Fred A. *The Organization and Administration of the Union Army, 1861–1865.* 2 vols. Cleveland: Arthur H. Clark Co., 1928.

Stackpole, Edward J. *Sheridan in the Shenandoah.* Harrisburg, Pa.: The Stackpole Co., 1961.

Tanner, Robert G. *Stonewall in the Valley: Thomas "Stonewall" Jackson's Shenandoah Valley Campaign Spring 1862.* Garden City, N.Y.: Doubleday, 1976.

Wert, Jeffrey D. *From Winchester to Cedar Creek: The Shenandoah Campaign of 1864.* Carlisle, Pa.: South Mountain Press, 1987.

Wiley, Bell I. *The Life of Billy Yank.* 1952. Reprint. Baton Rouge: Louisiana State University Press, 1978.

———. *The Life of Johnny Reb.* 1943. Reprint. Baton Rouge: Louisiana State University Press, 1978.

Williamson, Joel. *After Slavery: The Negro in South Carolina during Reconstruction 1861–1877.* Chapel Hill: University of North Carolina Press, 1965.

Index

"Dear Friend Anna"
was composed in 11½-point Garamond Number 3 leaded ½ point
on a Xyvision system with Linotronic output
by BookMasters, Inc.;
printed by sheet-fed offset
on 50-pound Glatfelter Natural acid-free stock
with halftones printed on 70-pound enamel stock,
Notch bound into binder's boards
covered with Holliston Kingston Natural cloth,
and wrapped with dustjackets printed in two colors
on 80-pound enamel and film laminated
by BookCrafters, Inc.;
designed by Will Underwood;
and published by
The University of Maine Press